WATER

THE CAN'T MISS SERIES

GARDENING
FOR THE SOUTH

Published by Cool Springs Press, a Division of Thomas Nelson, Inc., P.O. Box 141000, Nashville, Tennessee 37214.

Cataloging in Publication Data is available
ISBN: 1-5918-6150-0

First printing 2006
Printed in the United States of America
10 9 8 7 6 5 4 3 2 1

Managing Editor: Cindy Kershner
Cover Design: Becky Brawner, Unlikely Suburban Design
Book Design: Bruce Gore
Production Artist: S.E. Anderson
Cover Photo: Greg and Sue Speichert

Cool Springs Press books may be purchased in bulk for educational, business, fundraising, or sales promotional use. For information, please email SpecialMarkets@ThomasNelson.com.

Visit the Thomas Nelson website at **www.ThomasNelson.com** and the Cool Springs Press website at **www.coolspringspress.net**.

WATER

GARDENING
FOR THE SOUTH

THE CAN'T MISS SERIES

TERI
DUNN

COOL SPRINGS PRESS
A Division of Thomas Nelson Publishers
Since 1798

acknowledgements

Thanks to Ramona Wilkes, Cindy Kershner, Jenny Andrews, and Hank McBride; to Joe Tomocik, Anita Nelson, Kathy Hanes, and Karyn Dekker; to Donna Mello; to Dave Alvin, the King of California, and Tom Russell. And, as ever, thanks to *los tres amigos*.

Special thanks to the incomparable Paula Biles—a font of knowledge, creativity, professionalism, and good cheer.

This book is dedicated with love and appreciation to the memory of two great men, great friends, and great water gardeners: John Mirgon and W.C. (Bill) Frase.

—Teri Dunn

photography credits

Paula Biles: 3, 6, 7A, 7B, 9A, 12, 13, 18, 20A, 20B, 22A, 23A, 23B, 24, 31, 35A, 35B, 35C, 37B, 38, 39, 40A, 42, 48, 49, 50, 53, 54, 55, 57B, 60, 61, 62, 63, 64, 66, 67, 69, 70, 71, 72A, 72B, 72C, 75B, 77, 80, 83, 86, 91, 94A, 95, 100A, 101, 107, 116, 117, 120, 121, 127, 131, 133A, 133B, 134A, 135A, 138A, 140A, 140B, 141A, 143B, 144A, 146A, 148, 149B, 150A, 150B, 151B, 156A, 157B, 158B, 159A, 159B, 161A, 162, 164A, 164B, 165B

Jerry Pavia: 5, 9B, 11, 14, 22B, 34, 36, 37A, 40B, 47, 52, 56, 57A, 59, 87, 119, 124,

Joseph Tomocik: 46, 132, 134B, 142, 143A, 144B, 146B, 152, 153B, 156B, 158A, 160A, 160B, 161B, 163A

Florida Aquatic Nurseries: 88, 135B, 136A, 136B, 137A, 137B, 139A, 141B, 145A, 145B, 147A, 163B,

Anita Nelson: 19, 32A, 32B, 33, 73, 74, 75A, 92, 99, 138B, 147B, 151A,

Greg and Sue Speichert: 51, 65, 89A, 94B, 104, 114A, 114B, 118, 127, 149A, 153A,

Rosemary Kautzky: 44, 90, 93, 96, 97, 105, 109, 110, 112, 115, 123,

Thomas Eltzroth: 8, 10, 85, 139B, 157A

Liz Ball/Rick Ray: 76, 154A, 154B, 165A

John Meeks: 28A, 28B, 28C, 28D

Felder Rushing: 15, 100B, 155B,

Pam Harper: 155A

André Viette: 89B

contents

introduction

The Joys of Water Gardening

There's something so enchanting about water in a garden! Whether it's a quiet pool of colorful blooming waterlilies, a splashing fountain or tumbling waterfall, or simply a small tub of aquatic plants decorating a sunny corner of the patio, water always completely transforms the scene. It's captivating. Everyone who visits your yard is immediately drawn to the display. So are you, for a water garden has a primal attraction.

Pausing at the edge of your water garden, you will find that you, just as much as the plants and animals that dwell within, need water. A water garden restores us to nature's rhythms, allows us to contemplate the vastness of the sky, and reminds us of our importance…and our insignificance. Jarring noises and distractions drop away. In a busy and troubled world, something as simple as a backyard pond is a balm to the human spirit.

Taking the Plunge

You may have many questions before you get started. Is it difficult? Expensive? A lot of work? Can you dismantle or move a water garden if you have to? What must be done to get your display through the winter months? What about fish? Algae? Are there tricks for coaxing waterlilies to produce lots of glorious flowers? What other plants can you count on for colorful flowers and interesting foliage?

Rest easy—all these questions and more will be answered in the coming pages. The main thing you need to know at the outset is that water gardening is far easier and more satisfying than you may ever have imagined. You will be pleasantly surprised!

The Basics

A water garden may or may not look like a natural pond, depending on the mood you are striving for. But in practical terms, it is not like a pond

Water gardens come in all sorts, shapes, and sizes.

7

in nature. Most significantly, it does not have an inlet or outlet for the water such as a spring or stream or even groundwater. To help this controlled and finite environment succeed and look beautiful, you need to understand some basic principles. Experience has shown that attending to these items makes a great-looking and satisfying display possible and, indeed, easy.

Plentiful Sunshine

In order to grow well and to produce flowers, most aquatic plants—including waterlilies, lotuses, marginal plants, floating plants, and even submerged ones—need sun, and lots of it. At least six hours per day is good, and more is even better.

Sun also helps keep the water warm, which the plants enjoy. In the finite environment of a water garden, water will heat up naturally. In warm weather, water closer to the surface will be warmest, of course, while the deepest recesses of a pool will be cooler. Shallow water heats up faster and will be warmer during the day, something to keep in mind if you are growing tropical plants that relish higher temperatures.

This 'St. Louis Gold' waterlily is thriving in the sun.

Ample Space

Installing a water garden is an important and exciting investment. Taking waterlilies as an example, if it's an in-ground pond and you want to grow more than one waterlily, make it big—a 4-foot by 8-foot pool is a good starter size. If you are ambitious and want to have a variety of waterlilies, obviously your pond will need to be larger. Bear in mind, in the memorable words of one landscape contractor, "Nobody ever complained that their water garden was too large!"

That said, there are also numerous varieties of water plants suitable for smaller pools. And there are many charming water garden containers small enough for a deck or patio. Decide how much space you have for a pond and choose plants whose mature size is appropriate.

Depth is also important. Typically 18 to 24 inches is sufficient to meet the needs of most favorite water plants. Any deeper, and you may find it tricky to place and maintain pots of plants. A pool bottom gets slippery over time, too—a good reason to make access from the sides as easy as possible.

IF YOU BUILD IT, THEY WILL COME

One of the pleasures of having a water garden is observing unexpected but welcome visitors. This may send you running for your camera, or just give you some moments of hushed wonder. Among the creatures that may appear are:

- **dragonflies**
- **turtles**
- **butterflies**
- **hummingbirds**
- **frogs**
- **birds**

Occasionally visitors that you don't want (especially if you have fish) will appear, most notably herons and raccoons—for advice on fending off these pests, see Chapter 3.

Dragonflies are welcome visitors.

Balance

Though a contained environment, a home water garden can and should reach a desirable state of equilibrium. At that point, the water surface will be about two-thirds covered with floating and marginal plants. There will be some algae in the water, but not too much. Fish and perhaps a few scavenging freshwater snails will patrol the water and pool sides contently. (See Chapter 2 for information on stocking your pond.)

When a water garden or tub display is up and running and has reached this steady state, it is a real pleasure. You can stop and admire it, perhaps clipping off a spent leaf or two or an emerging waterlily blossom to bring indoors to a vase. But at least during the height of the growing season, it won't require a lot of effort—certainly no more than, say, a flowerbed in another part of your yard.

How long does it take to achieve this desirable steady state? It varies depending on the size and contents of your display, but it can take anywhere from six weeks to a few months. In the meantime, just keep an eye on things and attend to routine maintenance as needed (see Chapter 3 for details).

The fact is, you set the ecosystem in motion and monitor it, but nature takes its course. Just like any other form of garden, water gardening is a combination of human control and natural processes. You

Two-thirds of your water garden should be covered with plants.

yourself need to find a sense of balance, too, where you have the good sense to understand that you are not in full control, but are, in fact, a privileged steward.

Some Concerns for the South

Water gardening in a mild climate has many pluses. The pool liner or container is less likely to be damaged from freezing temperatures, but also the plants will really thrive. It is a wonderful and gratifying hobby especially well suited to the region.

A warm water temperature is a good thing for most plants and fish. But it also encourages faster breakdown and decay of spent foliage and flowers as well as fish waste, so you need to be tidy so that too much organic matter in the display doesn't become a problem.

High Humidity

High humidity, especially in the summer months, is par for the course. Plants of tropical origins are undaunted and indeed will grow and flower vigorously. If you include some hardy ones, and there's no reason why you shouldn't, you may discover that some struggle a bit. Signs that a plant is not enjoying the heavy, moisture-laden air include poor flowering and the appearance of fungal diseases—either remove or treat afflicted plants.

The South is a great area for water gardens.

Mosquitoes

Because these annoying biting insects reproduce in standing water, you need to take steps to prevent or discourage them. Adding fish to your garden pool is the easiest tactic. Many fish, from ordinary goldfish to ornamental koi, will eat mosquito larvae and thus keep the population under control. If you do not have fish, try "mosquito dunks," inexpensive donut-shaped objects that release a biological mosquito larvicide—these are available from water-garden suppliers and many garden centers.

A Long Growing Season

As with your entire garden, a water garden in a mild climate is productive over a long period—in

some areas, practically all year long. This multiplies your pleasure being outdoors. But it also means that you must be diligent with maintenance, especially pruning. Don't neglect your fish or let them become overpopulated. Continue to fertilize plants that appear to need the extra boost, and divide those that become overgrown, preferably in the "shoulder seasons" of late winter and fall.

Pest Plants

Because the climate and the warm water temperatures that go along with it are so encouraging to plant growth, naturally rampant growers can have a field day. One week there are a few plants, and the next there are way too many. In the case of floating and submerged ones, you should scoop out excess plants on a regular basis. Some marginals can grow aggressively, too, such as cattails—an important reason to always grow marginals in pots in home water gardens.

It is very important not to discard unwanted extras in a place where they can cause even more trouble, like a natural or manmade waterway. Instead, toss them on your compost pile or even dig them into your garden soil somewhere else on your property.

Despite the best efforts of diligent and well-meaning gardeners, some aquatic plants have gotten loose and ended up clogging rivers, streams, reservoirs, and lakes in the South. Often these are nonnative plants (originally imported from tropical regions of Asia or South or Central America), and they grow unchecked. As a result, some are now banned—you may not buy, grow, or transport these plants across state lines. If a water plant is not for sale at your local nursery, this is often the reason, so please don't cheat. There are always plenty of suitable substitutes in terms of plant size and flower color. (For more, please read Warning: Invasive Plants on page 82.)

Water lettuce is now banned in many parts the South.

RED ALERT

Owing to the plentiful hot, bright sunshine and long summer days, the color of red-flowered waterlilies and tropical plants is never as vibrant as you'd wish and fades fast. If you can provide a little shade for your water garden in the hottest, most stressful part of the day, you may still be able to enjoy these plants. Otherwise, there are plenty of other hot colors you can enjoy, from fiery orange to bright yellow.

Choosing
and Installing Your
.Water Garden

installing a water feature is a major decision—but it can also be one of the best and most exciting garden additions you ever make. If you choose your garden and its site wisely, the result will look fabulous and become your pride and joy. Also, as you will learn in the coming chapters, a properly installed and stocked water garden will *not* be high maintenance. So it behooves you to get the project off to a good start.

In this chapter, we'll look at the various sorts of water gardens you can install, from a charming container tucked into a nook to various types of full-fledged in-ground pools that can become a spectacular focal point in your landscape. Fountains, statuary, streams, waterfalls, special equipment, dramatic lighting, and other ideas will also be covered. You'll be able to get a clearer picture of what might work for you and what's involved in installing it.

How to Pick a Good Spot

Just as with installing a new flower garden or planting a new shrub or tree, it is critical to select an appropriate location somewhere in your yard. This "heads off at the pass" numerous potential problems, as you can imagine. It also gives you a chance to decide how best to show off your display.

Adjacent landscaping—including non-plant items— helps this water garden fit into its surroundings.

The Best Site
No matter whether it is large or small, sunk into the ground or raised above, a water garden always has the following basic requirements.

■ PLENTIFUL SUN: The majority of water plants adore full sun and bloom with gusto as a result—specifically, six or so hours per day. A spot that is suitable for a flowerbed or vegetable garden can easily host a water garden.

■ A SPOT FREE OF LARGE PLANTS: Especially trees and shrubs, which interfere from below with roots and from above with falling leaves and twigs.

■ OUT IN THE OPEN: The best spot is one with ample elbow room. You will be able to tend your water garden more readily and admire it more easily. Sufficient air circulation is also good for the health of the plants—and the fish.

■ A LEVEL SURFACE: This is important because water always responds to gravity and you don't want runoff or spillovers. Granted, few sites are

A LESS-THAN-PERFECT SITE

Not enough sun? If your chosen spot doesn't get the recommended six or so hours of sun each day, your choices will have some limitations, and you'll need to select shade-tolerant plants. Sun-loving waterlilies will not flower, but you can still include handsome "marginal" plants.

Not out in the open? A hidden or shaded spot can have the obvious drawback of not being the focal point you wished for. However, such a pool can instead become a pleasant garden surprise, a "secret garden." Do beware, however, of setting up one under shade trees . . . you'll constantly be removing leaves and other debris.

Not level? While you can try to shore up a sloping spot with rocks or gravel, or even soil, your efforts to make a rather steep location level might be doomed, sorry to say. Remember that a pool, once installed, is heavy with the weight of water and slumping can easily occur. You may also end up battling run-off from your yard and its effects (muddy water, for instance, or worse, fertilizers or garden chemicals), or struggling with drainage problems (including overflow out of the pool).

Sometimes the perfect site is easy to find—an open, sunny, level spot.

naturally *perfectly* level, but don't worry—it's easy to make the necessary minor adjustments during installation.

■ GOOD VISIBILITY: You will enjoy your water garden so much more, potentially at all times of the day and all seasons of the year, if you can view it easily from your house and/or patio or deck. (Being able to see it well is also a safety issue, just in case someone or something falls in!)

Ultimately, you want your water display to be a star in your landscape, or even the main focal point. Aside from the practical reasons described above, it is always more aesthetically pleasing to view one that is comfortable in its surroundings. Though technically artificial, it ought to look like it belongs. Choosing a spot where it can prosper will go a long way towards ensuring that.

The easiest way to pick a suitable spot is to walk around your yard with the above requirements in mind. You might discover that the best location is already occupied by something else, such as a grill, open lawn, an ornamental tree, or even an established flower garden.

Before you start moving things around and digging, try flagging the chosen spot to make absolutely sure this is what you want to do. Set a lawn chair on the spot, or outline the proposed pool with the garden hose, an outdoor electrical cord, or even a sprinkled line of flour.

(Or, if you have one, you can even lay a large mirror on the site—this idea is most practical, of course, for a smaller water garden, but is quite effective for envisioning its presence.) Leave the "place marker" there for a few days, observe it, and ponder your choice—especially from inside the house. Be sure the spot meets the criteria above and that you are willing and able to clear obstructions to make way for the new show.

Plan ahead because you may want to sit near your water garden.

Viewing the Water Garden

Your water garden should be in a spot where you and your visitors can see it easily. Bear in mind that part of the drama of a large water garden comes from viewing it from some distance, so it's possible to take in all of it at a glance. A small water garden can be charming tucked into a niche, garden room, or courtyard. This also creates an intimate, contemplative space; be sure to provide a seating area nearby. When you're inside, will the water feature be visible from windows or a sliding glass door? A good view from indoors can be especially important when the weather prevents you from being outside to enjoy it.

Being able to see it from an indoor vantage point is also practical. You'll know when birds, welcome or otherwise, visit. You'll be able to catch raccoons or muskrats in the act if these creatures decide to stop by (for advice on coping with these intruders, see Chapter 3).

WATER SPOTS

Here are some locations others have found suitable for their water gardens. Remember that up to six hours of direct sunlight is important, especially for blooming plants.

- beside a deck, or as part of a stepped-deck layout.
- just off the edge of a patio.
- next to a gazebo.
- next to (but with a few-feet buffer) a fence or wall.
- in the middle of the lawn.
- at the base of a slope (provided the ground levels out and does not naturally hold water since a low-lying, swampy area can be problematic—see Areas to Avoid).

A clear line of sight is an important safety consideration. If a neighbor, child, or curious pet should wander and fall into your pool, it is more likely that someone would be able to see and respond quickly. Garden pools aren't very deep, as a rule, but it doesn't take deep water for a child to drown.

Viewing it from outdoors is another matter. All of the above concerns will be factors when you stand on the back porch, deck, or patio, but you should also consider being able to view and enjoy your water garden from various spots around the property. For close-up viewing, a bench, some chairs, or even a picnic table nearby is nice, although, if your pool includes a fountain or waterfall, bear in mind that there will be splashing on windy days.

Finally, if you decide on a pond that is longer than it is wide, such as a kidney shape or rectangle, you have two options. Orient it so it is more readily and naturally viewed from a longer side (lengthwise). This gives the impression that it is bigger than it actually is, shows off plants to best advantage, and/or increases reflectivity. Alternatively, if you have a vista you want to direct the eye to, it makes more sense to orient the pool so the shorter side is facing the viewer.

All of these viewing considerations can be evaluated before you install. Just use the advice above—that is, mark the chosen spot and observe it from various angles, from indoors and out, at various times of day, for at least a few days.

Areas to Avoid

In nature, ponds are often located in low-lying places. They are fed by the local water table, streams, and rain. An area in your yard that naturally collects water might overflow your pond on a regular basis when it rains or make the pond the recipient of run-off, and water accumulating under the liner will cause it to bubble up. If your yard has a swampy, low-lying area, consider turning it into a bog garden. Many of the "marginal" plants suitable for water gardens prosper in such a setting—see Chapter 4.

Another important "don't": Don't install a pond in an area with trees and shrubs. Not only do these create shade that inhibits flowering and good pool health, they also shed leaves and twigs and maybe even spent flowers, fruit, or nuts. If such larger plants are close by, you may also make the unpleasant discovery that their roots are in your way when you begin to dig. So site your display well away from them.

Finally, a water garden really doesn't belong on a slope or hillside. It can be done, with a lot of shoring up and the inclusion of diversion channels so unwanted water doesn't flow in. But the weight may cause your efforts to backslide or slump after a while. While a pool could still, in theory, be installed in a tricky location with the help of professional pond builders, in the end, you're much better off picking a relatively flat area.

Other Practical Considerations

There are just a few more things you might need to consider before you commit yourself to installing a water garden in a certain spot, though these issues won't apply in every case.

1. If you are planning to install something that runs on electricity (a pump, fountain, or night lighting, for instance), there should be a direct-as-possible line between the chosen spot and the outlet/house. Note also that outdoor wiring needs to be protected by a "GFCI" or "GFI" ("ground fault circuit interrupter" or "ground fault interrupter"), an extension-cord style device that automatically shuts off power when it detects a leak in the electrical current, thus preventing shock.

2. Do not plan a water garden in an area where there are—or might be—underground cables, pipes, sewer lines, or a septic field. These can be obstructions or worse, safety hazards. Plus your display could potentially block access to them. So check a survey of your property, or have someone knowledgeable check. (Utility companies provide this service free of charge.)

3. Although plentiful sunlight is always advised for flowering aquatics, some shade may be good. This is especially true in the case of smaller ponds, because they can really heat up . . . and hot water is stressful to certain plants and fish.

4. Position the pond where you will be able to admire it while sitting, either indoors or out. While it's fine for you or visitors to stand pondside and admire everything, it's more relaxing to have nearby seating (benches or other outdoor furniture).

5. Some towns and cities require a permit for a water garden, particularly if it will be deeper than the typical 18 to 24 inches, or if it

Don't install a pond in an area with trees and shrubs. Not only do these create shade that inhibits flowering and good pool health, they also shed leaves and twigs and maybe even spent flowers, fruit, or nuts.

A little shade can be all right for the plants you want to grow, although most will want six hours of sun.

will be sited in a front yard or other spot that is visible or accessible to foot traffic passing by. You can still install the pool you want, but you may be required to put up a fence.

GOING UNDERGROUND

If you're planning an in-ground display, invasive tree or shrub roots are common obstacles. But there are other equally important concerns.

Always check the soil first before committing yourself to a spot. Take a stab at it with a good, sharp shovel, then dig down about a foot. If you encounter hardpan or lots of rocks, it might not be such a good location. Not only will you, or the contractor you hire, have an arduous digging job ahead, but ground that is impervious or riddled with potentially sharp obstructions is not very welcoming to a liner.

The soil in your chosen spot should also drain well. If you quickly hit water upon digging the exploratory hole, ground water can get under your pool, leading to "bubbles" that are, at best, unsightly and at worst, stress the liner. Water bubbles under a liner can also cause objects that you add to your pool—from potted plants to statuary—to fall over.

Last but not least, make sure you're not planning to dig into utility, water, or electrical pipes or lines. When in doubt, call your local provider, who will be glad to come out and check the area at no charge.

DRAW IT

You don't have to be a professional to at least come up with a rough "bird's-eye view" sketch. Just try to make it to scale, using graph paper if need be (if you have one, a property survey map will be very useful). Or, photograph the intended spot, take it to a print shop and get it blown up larger, then draw on this with a grease pencil. Alternatively, invest in some of the landscaping software now available—some do include "pond elements." No matter what method you choose, this step will give you an important opportunity to picture your new water garden more accurately.

Deciding Dimensions

When you want to put in a more substantial water garden than a mere tub or container, you need to begin by figuring out the size that you want, and whether it will fit.

The first rule of water-garden size is actually the same rule that landscapers use when recommending the installation of a new flowerbed. It needs to be in scale. That is, it should neither be too big for its surroundings nor too tiny. If it is much too large, the water feature will overwhelm the area and look out of place, instead of bringing your wished-for atmosphere of beauty and repose. If it is too tiny, it will get lost in the crowd of other plants and other garden features.

Style Issues

Give some thought to the kind of personality you want your water garden to have. Ideally it should be a match not only for your house's architecture but also for the rest of your property as well. It can set the tone for your garden, or a major part of it. Or it can become the finishing touch.

It's equally important that your water garden match your lifestyle and how you plan to enjoy it. Will it be a private retreat or a place to entertain guests? The style and layout of the rest of your garden, as it is now or as you envision it, should give you an answer.

Although "formal" and "informal" styles are frequently divergent, at least in theory, this is your garden. If you prefer to mix elements and principles, or come up with your own hybrid design, go ahead. The following discussion is intended to show you some traditional options.

Finally, draw inspiration from water gardens you've seen, even if only in photos. Many approaches and styles have been used throughout history and still have an influence today—Moorish, Italian, French, Japanese, and

Outline the water garden before you begin to dig.

contemporary American examples, to name but a few. From the very formal, flat, glassy planes of water at Tuscany's Villa Gamberaia to the lush, almost overgrown look of Monet's water garden at Giverny, France, water has found a home in many forms and many places. With thought and planning, yours will fit into and bring great beauty to your landscape as well.

Formal water gardens can look very different from each other.

Formal Water Gardens

These obviously are best suited to more formal surroundings. A formal water garden can be a good choice for a smaller garden, where a strong

Statues—of everything from an Aquarius figure to water nymphs to a gazing ball on a pedestal—are attractive additions for formal water garden displays. Choose quality pieces touted for their ability to withstand wind and weather for a long time. Avoid anything made out of or containing limestone, which can disintegrate over time and leach into the water below. And remember to provide strong anchoring support (even if it's out of sight in the water) for your figurines, so you don't have to climb into the water periodically to right them.

hand on the overall design looks better. Think of the courtyard fountains of Spain and other European countries and Mexico, for example, or even just a small city garden. Very large, expansive properties can also be compatible with a formal-style display.

Formal water gardens tend to be based on a geometric or symmetrical shape: a square, rectangle, or perfect circle. The emphasis may be mainly on the reflections in the water surface. A fountain or some statuary is often added. In such cases, you have to sacrifice the number and variety of plants you install. On the other hand, you'll enjoy the graceful appearance, musical sound, and a dramatic focal point. You'll also be better able to enjoy the reflections in the water's surface. You needn't eliminate plants altogether. You can enjoy "a splash of nature"—just make sure that the plants you include are secondary to the artifice your formal pool displays. Note that formal pools also use regular, neat edging materials, such as bricks, blocks, and tiles.

"Monoculture" plantings, such as using only waterlilies, seem to have a more formal air. Alternatively, create a monochromatic planting scheme, using all-white flowers, for instance, or all lavender.

If you decide to site your formal water garden in a spot with less-than-ideal amounts of sunlight, you'll have to forgo waterlilies and perhaps some other flowering aquatics. But you can make quite an elegant display of intriguing green-foliage plants or some variegated-leaved ones.

Informal Water Gardens

Informal garden pools are more casual in shape and more versatile for planting schemes of all kinds. Landscaping tastes seem to run in cycles, and these days the "natural" look is popular (though the wise gardener knows that even a "wild" effect requires effort). Pools in various irregular shapes, such as kidney, teardrop, lagoon, and "amoeba," are just a few of the ones you can either buy pre-formed or create. Once established, they can give the impression that they've always been there.

To give your informal garden that desirable "settled" look, take a cue from nature. Ponds in nature are a continuum from plants floating in deeper

Informal garden pools are more casual in shape and more versatile for planting schemes of all kinds.

water, to plants growing in shallow water, to plants growing on the banks. This transitional effect is easy to imitate. Place plants on your pool's side shelves (preformed liners often come with these shelves), or raise them up on a support. Then grow moisture-loving plants of compatible appearance alongside your pool, such as arching ferns or a small Japanese maple with a graceful profile. (For more plant suggestions, see Chapter 4, Plant Directory.)

Informal pools can be successfully accented with certain fountain designs or a simple waterfall. A rock waterfall will look better, by the way, if the rocks are a locally occurring material and there are other rocks in the nearby landscape.

The sheer variety of plants appropriate for an informal pool immediately supplies a lush, natural look. Feel free to experiment by combining various colors, leaf forms, and textures. When waterlilies and other aquatic plants that float or trail on the water's surface are offset by what professional landscape designers call "vertical accents" supplied by marginal plants, your pool will be full of variety and interest.

Just be careful not to overdo. A too-full pool can become an unnatural looking hodgepodge, too busy, and not restful to the eye whether seen from a distance or up close.

Types of Water Gardens

If you are new to water gardening and just want to dip your toe in (so to speak!), you may wish to start small, with a display that is more of a "garden accent." Or, you may have specific landscaping plans in mind and have no qualms about installing a substantial pool that will be the star of the show. Below are the most common options: container/tub, in-ground (you may use either pre-formed shell or lay a special plastic sheet into free-form shape), and aboveground—all with or without additions like a fountain, waterfall, or cascade/streambed.

Container Water Garden Displays

SMALL IS BEAUTIFUL: Creative gardeners have come up with the most ingenious and charming little displays. You might want to try one as a garden accent (instead of or in addition to a more substantial water garden). Almost any watertight container can be used. An umbrella stand, filled with water, can host a taro, a papyrus, and/or a water-loving iris. A small bowl or kettle perched on a deck or patio can show off some duckweed, water lettuce, or a lovely mosaic plant (which arrays small diamond-shaped leaves on the water's surface).

The kind of container enhances the mood of your water garden.

WORDS OF CAUTION

Small containers tend to heat up. While certain plants of tropical origin may not mind, others might just cook. You can help by replacing or topping off with cool water from time to time, and/or making sure the container is not out in full, blazing sun all day long.

Also, the larger your container is, the heavier it will be. So put it in its spot *before* filling it with water and plants. And be prepared to empty it out completely if you decide you want to move it to another spot—either that, or drain it down a few inches to prevent sloshing and use a dolly or the wheeled bases other plants, such as a potted tree, are on.

Grouping two or more containers gives you the ease of container gardening but covers more space.

TUB GARDENS: Some nurseries offer these as kits that include a suitable, attractive container and a selection of plants—some to pot up, some to scatter and let float. Or you can simply buy any nice watertight container that appeals to you, ceramic or plastic, and make your own. Do-it-yourselfers have also used half whiskey barrels (lined with black plastic or a fitted plastic insert), but there are lots of attractive new alternatives that abound at well-stocked garden centers and in specialty catalogs.

SUNKEN CONTAINERS: Taking a container and sinking it in the ground is a simple and ingenious way to have a small in-ground water garden. Just remember to allow a lip a few inches *above* the ground's surface or you'll be contending with run-off problems. You can disguise the edge if need be with plants or edging materials such as stone.

MIXING IT UP: Even a small water garden ought to be a balanced ecosystem, so that all you have to do is install it, enjoy it, and groom it occasionally. A blend of submerged plants, floating plants, and upright marginal plants and/or a waterlily adds up to a good group, as practical as they are attractive. (For more on establishing balance, consult Chapter 2.)

WATERLILIES IN TIGHT QUARTERS: Since a waterlily needs to grow in soil in a pot, the pool needs to be big enough to accommodate that pot…in other words, a larger water feature will be necessary. Obviously your best choices for a small display are waterlilies that are dwarf, which affects root-ball size, the ambitions of the spreading lilypads, and flower size. Seek out waterlilies that are described as "small," "mini," or "dwarf" (see the listings in Chapter 4). However, a number of waterlilies normally considered "medium-sized" will adapt well to a smaller pot and grow into a correspondingly smaller plant. (For more ideas and details, please see Chapter 2.) At any rate, such a display is a real conversation piece, on a patio, deck, flanking a front door, or any other prominent sunny spot.

FISH IN SMALL CONTAINERS: Fish can live quite happily in a container garden, but be aware that you will probably need to treat tap (municipal) water before you add them. If you garden in an area where mosquitoes live, be advised that they adore any body of stagnant, still water, which can become ready-made breeding grounds. One solution is to include mosquito-eating fish in your tub garden (guppies or goldfish). For more fish information, see Chapter 2.

Setting Up a Container Garden

CHOOSE AN APPROPRIATE CONTAINER. For plants to survive and prosper, it's best to have something that is not too small. If you wish to include at least one waterlily, a good typical starter size is 18 to 24 inches deep and wide. If you're only planning on marginals or floaters, narrower and shallower can work. In any case, just be sure that the container is watertight!

CHOOSE AN APPROPRIATE SPOT. It should be level. If you plan to use flowering plants, the site should receive six or so hours of sun each day. It's

Fish can live quite happily in a container garden, but be aware that you will probably need to treat tap (municipal) water before you add them.

helpful, but not mandatory, that the site be within reach of a hose, so you can top off the water level easily when you lose it to evaporation.

FILL IT WITH WATER. Tap, or hose, water is fine—just be aware that municipalities these days tend to treat their water with chlorine or chloramines, chemicals that you should allow to dissipate for a day or so before adding plants and/or fish. (A water-garden supplier can sell you tablets that neutralizes chloramines.) Don't fill all the way to the top, because whatever plants you add will displace some water. Another good reason to let it sit for a bit is to give the water a chance to warm up—many aquatic plants appreciate warmer water.

ADD PLANTS FIRST, FISH LAST. Potted plants can be elevated at various heights on bricks or other sturdy supports. Fish should go in at the end, so they are not in your way and don't get harmed as you work. For more details on stocking a container garden, consult Chapter 2.

In-ground Pools

PREPARING THE SITE: Assuming you have chosen a suitable site, the job now comes down to clearing it and digging down. Generally speaking, you want to excavate wider and deeper than the actual pool will be. Wider, so that it will be easier to install edging material, and deeper, so you can line the bottom of the hole with a buffer of several inches of sand, heavy landscape fabric, or special "underlayment" fabric sold for this purpose (sometimes it's called "geotextile" fabric). Be thorough and neat—take your time and do the job right.

COPING WITH TERRAIN: If your site is not perfectly flat, and even if it is, you should do a little tinkering at the time of installation to give your display the best possible chance of success and ease of care. To keep out run-off from your yard, gently grade away from the pool's edges. If the site has a slight slope to it, a berm or retaining wall on the downside will be necessary and a drainage trench on the uphill side is recommended.

ALLOWING FOR A SIDE SHELF: Whether you design and dig the hole yourself or purchase and set in a preformed liner, a shelf that goes around the inside perimeter of the pool may be desirable. It has a practical function—it allows you easier access to the pool, should you need to enter it to add or care for plants. And its purpose is also aesthetic—you can array pots of plants that enjoy shallower water along its length. A width of about 12 inches is best, and the shelf should be around 8 to 12 inches below the finished water level.

There are a few drawbacks to shelves. They do take space away from the total water volume. And predators and pests can use them to gain easier access to the pool.

LINER OPTIONS

Pre-formed liners

Rigid plastic or, where you can find them, fiberglass liners come in a variety of shapes, sizes, and depths, with and without shelves of varying widths. They're usually 18 inches deep, which is sufficient for any water plants you might wish to grow, including waterlilies. A typical one is made of sturdy polyethylene plastic.

Pros: Easy to install, easy to clean. Resists puncture damage. Longer-lasting. Smaller ones can be fairly inexpensive.

Cons: Larger ones can be expensive. Needs to be perfectly level and well supported, or it can buckle.

Flexible liners

Special thick plastic (usually EPDM or butyl rubber) that you can position in any size or shape of hole you wish to create a water-garden display.

Pros: The size and shape is *your* choice! It's easier to conceal the edges from view because they are not rigid. Foot for foot, medium and large ponds lined with this material are cheaper than pre-formed.

Cons: Not as long lasting, can puncture more easily. Also, installation is more difficult.

Concrete

Ideally a 1:2:3 mix of gravel, sand, and Portland cement, poured quickly and seamlessly into a prepared hole in one day; reinforcing mesh and rods as well as a drain in the bottom are all advisable. (Swimming-pool contractors can do this job, if the project is too daunting to do yourself.)

Pros: Extremely tough, durable, long-lasting. Basically permanent. Not vulnerable to sunlight.

Cons: Expensive, and even more so if you hire someone to install it for you. Cracks and leaks (a risk in climates with freezing winters) are difficult and frustrating to seal. Unless your soil is heavy and packed, heaving can also become a problem in regions with cold winters.

There are a few drawbacks to shelves, however. They do take space away from the total water volume. And predators and pests can use them to gain easier access to the pool. Finally, it's not easy to create them yourself, making them the right dimensions and stable. So by all means weigh these concerns against the benefits and make the choice that is right for you.

LINER OPTIONS—PRE-FORMED OR FLEXIBLE: Ah, the moment of truth. You do have a choice of materials. Rigid plastic and more flexible rubber are justly popular materials and can last a long time (though not forever); it is wise to invest in quality material in order to get maximum mileage. In

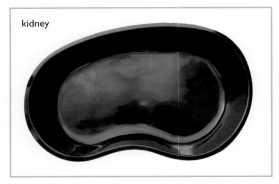
kidney

"Japanese" with side shelves

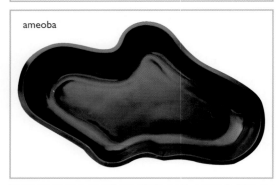
ameoba

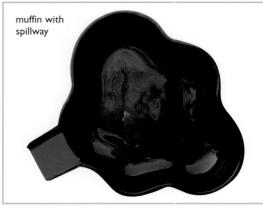
muffin with spillway

There are a number of different shapes available in pre-formed pools.

particular, seek out good UV-resistance because exposure to sunlight weakens plastic and causes it to become brittle over time. Cement liners are no longer as popular as they once were, thanks to the ease, convenience, and lower cost of the plastics, but may still be worth considering if you garden in a mild climate and want something permanent. To discover which kind is right for you, consult the liner options chart.

Pre-formed Options

If you go shopping for a pre-formed pool liner, you will find plenty of choices. They tend to be strong, rigid black plastic or fiberglass. You may see ones with full or partial shelves, ones with stream configurations or waterfall lips, round ones, kidney-shaped ones, teardrops, and so on. They can be 2, 3, or even 5 feet across and 6 feet or longer; one thing to bear in mind is that even the bigger ones seem somehow much smaller than you imagined once they're in place, full of plants, and with their edges hidden from view by stones, bricks, soil, or other material.

Pre-formed pool depths range from 9 to 18 inches. The deeper ones are recommended if you plan to grow waterlilies. The main drawback to shallower ones is that they are likely to get very hot in the summer, which can be stressful for some plants and fish. And they freeze solid in cold winters, so you'll need to plan on emptying these each fall (for details, see Chapter 3, Winterizing, page 95).

As for prices, good-quality liners typically range between $100 and $500. Mail-order suppliers, of course, tack on a shipping charge. The good thing is: no assembly required!

Finishing Touches

Once a pool is installed, the exposed edge needs to be covered and hidden from view. Your options include bricks, stones or pavers, tiles, wood, and soil . . . with or without plants. Or an overhanging deck or bridge.

This final step is more than just aesthetic. Covering over the rim helps anchor the liner in place, prevents run-off, helps integrate the pool into the surrounding landscape, and protects the plastic from

DO YOU NEED HELP?

While it's not a big deal to install a small display, the larger and more elaborate your plans are, the more likely it is that you are going to need help. Perhaps you just need someone with a shovel and a strong back to dig the hole and help you maneuver the liner in place. Or perhaps you'd like to hire a designer to make the necessary plans on paper and then execute everything yourself. Just remember that, in any event, another pair of eyes is always good to help you judge both the chosen spot and its suitability.

Complex displays, especially those involving waterfall installation, pumps, lighting, and the necessary electrical wiring or those that feature more than one pool, do tend to require professional help. It's well worth the investment, unless you are confident of your construction skills and have the time and energy required. To find qualified help, ask around. Anyone with an already-installed water garden that you've admired ought to be able to point you to his or her contractor (as well as give you any tips they learned along the way). Nurseries that carry water plants, supplies, and fish sometimes also offer installation services, sometimes as a package deal with the necessary supplies! But get references and go look at their completed projects, just to be sure they do good work and previous customers are happy. Another good way to find someone is to seek out a local pond club; if they offer tours, by all means, go on one. In any event, once you settle on qualified help, be prepared to pay a substantial hourly wage—these folks not only have to cover their labor, but insurance and equipment costs.

And remember, no matter who does the installation, if it is done right, in a good spot, it is a one-time expense. Like putting in a new flower border or even erecting a gazebo, the biggest effort is always at the outset.

exposure to the sun's damaging rays. If done properly so that it is sturdy and secure, it also gives you a place to kneel when you come to visit or work on the display.

A few tips, then:

■ Flat pavers or flagstones can overhang the water by an inch or two. More than that (without the support of mortar, that is), and they may wobble too much.

■ Don't let heavy materials press down directly on the liner's rim, which can damage the walls. Seat them in a few inches of mortar instead.

■ If you do use mortar, let it cure after mixing and installing. Otherwise, lime can leach into your pool and harm plants and fish. (For ways to cure, consult the back of the bag.)

■ If you fold over the liner, allow about 6 extra inches to avoid slippage; you can hide this excess behind rocks. Use edging with some texture to it so it won't be too slippery when wet if it accumulates a film of algae.

MATERIALS/TOOLS

- sharp, sturdy shovels
- wheelbarrow
- pruners
- carpenter's level, string level, or laser level
- straight, unwarped boards (2 x 4s work well)
- builder's sand or landscape fabric such as "underlayment" fabric (for cushioning the base)
- trowel
- hose

1. **Clean the liner.** Store-bought liners may have a dusty or chemical residue inside, so scrub or wipe out the interior.

2. **Set it on the chosen site.** Note that the sides are slightly angled to prevent them from buckling or caving in, so your hole will need to reflect this shape. Stand back and assess once more whether you like how it fits into your overall garden design, and make any last-minute adjustments.

3. **Trace the outlines on the ground.** You need two outlines—the top edge, which is further out, and the inner/bottom shape, which is within. The result will be a shape-within-a-shape design. Use some garden hoses, lengths of rope, outdoor electrical cords, or non-toxic spray paint (such as that used to mark boundaries on playing fields for sports—sporting goods stores and hardware stores sell this product) or even lines of sprinkled flour. Alternatively, with more digging but less precision, you can opt to simply dig one big hole that will accommodate the entire shape, and do more backfilling. Then move the liner out of your way. *Optional: A clever way to mark and monitor pool boundaries is to drive in stakes around the perimeter every 12 to 18 inches, perhaps 6 or 12 inches outside of the hole to be dug. You can make sure they're all level with one another before you even begin to dig.*

4. **Cut out the outlined area.** Use the edge of a shovel to excavate a shallow outline of the outer edge of your pool. If you're working on lawn, peel away the sod in pieces and save it to use as patches elsewhere in your yard or toss face-down on the compost pile. *Tip: Excavate an additional 6 inches wider than the outer boundary, just to allow yourself some flexibility in positioning the liner.*

5. **Excavate from the outer boundary down to the inner one.** Try your best to match the angle of the liner....'a good rule of thumb is to angle inward at 55 to 70 degrees towards the pool's bottom. But don't worry if it isn't perfect, as good backfilling later will allow you to make the necessary adjustments.

6. **Haul away soil as you work.** Use the wheelbarrow and do this often. There are many reasons for this practice— it gives you a break from digging, it gives you more elbow room, it spares the adjacent lawn from being damaged or smothered, and it saves you from having to face a big job at the project's end. Topsoil might be put to good use elsewhere in your garden, while subsoil can be used to make berms around the completed pool or piled up as a foundation for a waterfall, if desired. Discard all rocks and debris, and use pruners to clip out any roots you may encounter. *Tip: Reserve enough wheelbarrows of subsoil for backfilling at project's end, and topsoil for creating planting areas at the perimeter of the pond.*

7. **Dig the bottom a bit deeper, and smooth it.** Dig about 3 inches deeper than the actual pool depth. The bottom of the hole ought to be completely level (so that the top of the pool and the rim all the way around will be level). Firm the dirt in the bottom of the hole by stamping on it and/or tamp it down with the back of the shovel or a block of wood. Smooth it further with a piece of lumber. Just remember your goal here is a firm and evenly packed base to support the heavy water-filled pool. Also, carefully check the surface of the hole for any sharp objects now, before it's too late. (Once the pool is in place and filled, the pressure of the water on the liner will push hard against anything it's lying on in the bottom or sides of the hole, resulting in punctures.)

8. **Make sure the top is level.** If the site is level to begin with, chances are this will not be a problem. Check by laying a board across the entire hole (if the hole is too wide,

erect a stick in the middle and use two boards) and use a carpenter's level. Or simply use a laser level. If it's not level, add or remove soil from the ground's surface/pool edges, until you get it right. (This is easier than altering the depth of your hole.)

9. **Lay a base in the bottom of the hole.** Pour in and spread out several inches of builder's sand. The pool will sit more easily in the hole now and respond better to fine-tuning. The base also helps cushion the liner from punctures caused by any sharp objects you might have missed, or from the intrusion of rocks that migrate upward in the soil over the course of a cold-climate winter. Make the base even thicker if you want the pool to be slightly elevated in the hole to prevent runoff from entering it. (Alternative base materials include a layer of landscape or underlayment fabric, old carpet remnants, flattened cardboard boxes, or even a half-inch of damp newspapers.)

10. **Position the pool in the hole.** Wiggle the pool into position, and check once again to be sure it is level all along the rim. You can remove the liner temporarily to see whether it has made a level impression in the sand base and add more sand if necessary. (If you've used some other base material, it will be harder to be as precise.) Take your time with this step; you won't regret it.

11. **Now, add water.** Set the hose in the bottom of the pool and start trickling water in. When it's about a foot deep,

check for levelness once again. If you haven't been careful or something's gone awry, you'll have to stop, bail out the water, and return to steps 8, 9, and 10. (Of this onerous job, the English garden writer Nigel Colborn once remarked, "A dry liner is merely awkward to handle; a wet one is about as maneuverable as a beached pilot whale!")

12. **Fill the gaps all around.** While the water is slowly filling the liner, keep working! Using your hands and/or a trowel, scoop soil in around the sides (because the hole, as you dug it, is slightly too big for the pool). Tamp it very firmly and evenly in place so there are no gaps or air pockets. Work your way around a few times until the gap is evenly packed all sides. This equalizes the pressure between the water and the soil and prevents bulges. If you've elevated the rim a bit, be sure to pack in soil to support that part, too.

13. **Conceal the pool's lip.** You may do this now or later, but the object is both to hide from view and further anchor the exposed edges. Paving stones, bricks, and/or plants should do the trick. (See Finishing Touches, page 28.)

14. **Let the water sit.** Municipal (tap) water has been treated, at minimum with chlorine. While this kills bacteria and makes for safe drinking, it is not safe for fish and some plants. Luckily, it tends to evaporate in a day or two, so avoid the temptation to stock your pool immediately. Another reason to wait is that hose water may be chilly and letting it sit in the new pool for a couple of days allows it to warm up, making it more welcoming to plants and fish alike. *Note: If your town already uses chloramines to treat its water (as mandated by the EPA and slowly taking effect nationwide), a chemical neutralizer may be necessary—check with your local water department for details and advice. Chloramines are like salts and do not dissipate over time like chlorine. If not neutralized, they can remain indefinitely.*

Although you can see the edge of this preformed liner, it's not obtrusive.

MATERIALS/TOOLS

- sharp, sturdy shovels
- wheelbarrow
- pruners
- carpenter's level, string, or laser level
- straight, unwarped boards (2 x 4s work well)
- builder's sand, landscape fabric, or "underlayment" fabric (for cushioning the base)
- trowel
- hose
- 4- to 6-inch nails
- hammer
- rocks, bricks, or wood (for securing the sides)

1. **Calculate pool size.** This requires some simple math, so if math is not your forte, ask for help or have somebody double-check your calculations. The basic formula is length x width x depth. Remember to overestimate so you have plenty of overlap—better safe than sorry! Obviously a 5 x 8 foot pond will require more than a 5 x 8 foot liner. Here's what to do: For both length and width, add an extra 2 feet on all four sides (using this example, you're now up to 9 x 12 feet of plastic). Now you have to accommodate your pool's maximum depth, typically 18 inches…simply double it, meaning 18 inches x 2 = 36 inches or 3 feet. Add this number to both the length and width (using this 5 x 8-foot example, you now know you need a piece 12 x 15 feet).

2. **Go liner-shopping.** You want a big piece of black plastic or rubber, ideally to a durable thickness of 45 millimeters. The most popular choice is EPDM, but you may also consider a sheet of PVC, HDPE, or butyl rubber. A water-garden center or well-stocked home store will have materials in rolls and can cut a piece to your specifications. (Alternatively, you can order what you need from a water-garden catalog; give them a call and go over the specs, price, and shipping costs—which can be quite high because the plastic is heavy.) Store it out of the weather until installation day.

3. **Outline your shape.** Use a garden hose, outdoor electrical cord, flour, or spray paint formulated for outdoor use (available from hardware and sporting-supply stores). Remember, with this type of liner, you are free to make any shape you like, though simpler ones are obviously easier to execute.

Get help when installing a flexible liner.

4. **Dig the hole.** Stay within your established boundaries, but angle the sides so they gently slope (a 55- to 75-degree angle is standard). Allow for full or partial side shelves, if desired—about a foot wide is good, and they should be 8 to 12 inches below the finished water level. Also, you want to dig a few inches deeper than the pool's planned depth, to allow for a cushioning base layer.

5. **Haul away soil as you work.** Use the wheelbarrow and do this often. There are many reasons for this practice— it gives you a break from digging, it gives you more elbow room, it spares the adjacent lawn from being damaged or smothered, and it saves you having to face a big job at the project's end. Topsoil might be put to good use elsewhere in your garden, while subsoil can be used to make berms around the completed pool or piled up as a foundation for a waterfall, if desired. Discard all rocks and debris, and use pruners to clip out any roots you may encounter. But don't haul all of the soil away—reserve enough wheelbarrow loads to use around the perimeter of the pool when you're finished to hide the edges of the liner and create planting places for waterside plants.

6. **Check that the hole is level.** Check the top edges. If it is not level, adjust the ground by berming up soil.

7. **Warm up the liner.** On the day you intend to install it, take out the liner, unroll it flat, and let the sun warm it for a few hours. This makes it more supple and easier to handle. *Tip: Lay it on dirt or pavement, taking care not to damage it in any way. Laying it on the lawn may be tempting, but you could cook the grass underneath!*

8. **Prepare the base.** Thoroughly pack down the base as flat as possible with your shoes and/or the back of a shovel, then finish using a piece of board. Leave no sharp objects or obstructions that could puncture your liner later. Then pour in several inches of builder's sand or lay down some other base material, and smooth it out. Some flexible liners have a geotextile backing, so there's less need for underlayment. *Tip: This is your opportunity to make the bottom slope slightly to one side or a corner—which makes cleaning out debris later, when the pool is up and running, much easier because it will accumulate in that area, whether you sweep or drain to clean.*

9. **Maneuver the liner in place.** For this, you are likely to need several helpers—large liners are quite heavy, plus maneuvering it is much easier with extra pairs of hands. Drape it over the pool's cavity, taking care to distribute it evenly. Smooth it out, removing as many wrinkles as you can—this takes patience. There should be excess on all sides,

The flexible liner is the invisible part of this water garden.

but do not trim it yet! Temporarily tack down the edges with nails, then further anchor them with rocks or bricks.

10. **Start filling with water.** Place a hose into the middle of your pool and run it on low so it doesn't whip around. Some creases in the bottom and sides are inevitable, though the pressure of the water should flatten them. Patrol the sides as the pool fills, and gently tug or tweak where necessary.

11. **Lay down an edging.** Use rocks, bricks, wood, tile, wood, or pavers, and overlap the lip of the pool a bit, that is, let it hang out slightly over the side. This holds the excess plastic in place and also hides it from view. (See Finishing Touches, page 28.) If the edging is to be permanent, be sure to use material that has some texture to it so it won't be too slippery when it's wet or accumulates some algae.

12. **Trim excess plastic.** Be conservative. You still want some overlap on the top of the ground—heaven forbid you trim off too much and water is able to seep between the lining and the side of the hole!

13. **Let the water sit.** Municipal (tap) water has been treated, at minimum with chlorine. While this kills bacteria and makes for safe drinking, it is not safe for fish and some plants. Luckily, it tends to evaporate in a day or two, so avoid the temptation to stock your pool immediately. Another reason to wait is that hose water may be chilly and letting it sit in the new pool for a couple of days allows it to warm up, making it more welcoming to plants and fish alike. *Note: If your town already uses chloramines to treat its water (as mandated by the EPA and slowly taking effect nationwide), a chemical neutralizer may be necessary—check with your local water department for details and advice. Chloramines are like salts and will not dissipate over time like chlorine; if not neutralized they can remain indefinitely.*

EDGING DO'S AND DON'TS

Do: Make sure edging materials are secure and stable, to prevent anyone from falling in.

Don't: Don't simply lay a rock necklace over a liner on the ground. This won't really hide all of the liner from view, nor will it be especially strong or anchoring.

Do: In the case of flexible liners, stack rocks or other materials down from the edge right into the water; this is much more stabilizing.

Don't: Don't install plants around the outside of the pool until you've completed planting and stocking the interior—otherwise, you'll be constantly trampling or sitting on them.

The right kind of edging adds to the beauty of your formal water garden.

Aboveground Pools

No digging required! Water gardens that are not sunken but rather sit on a surface—the ground, a patio, courtyard, terrace, or deck—are yet another option. Larger than a container or tub garden (discussed above) but smaller than most in-ground pools, aboveground ones are increasingly popular.

A raised pool is also a good option if your yard has heavy clay or rocky soil, any ground that would be difficult to dig in.

PROS:

■ SAFETY: A child or pet is much less likely to fall in.

■ ACCESSIBILITY: From those who simply want to spare their backs to gardeners in wheelchairs, raised displays are easy to maintain.

■ ON THE LEVEL: It should be easy to make sure the display is level—just set it up on an already-level surface. And run-off from the surrounding landscape will never be a problem.

■ VIEWING PLEASURE: You can appreciate your plants at close range and get eye to eye with your pet fish.

■ LOCATION: It is easy to find a good location since you don't need to worry about tree roots, hard-to-dig or rocky soil, or power lines underground.

CONS:

■ LIMITED SEASONALITY: Even with insulation around the sides, the display may not be able to carry on through the winter months in colder climates. This means you will have to empty it in the fall.

■ WEIGHT: Depending on where you display it, the garden's weight—with water in it—can be a problem if your deck or patio is not sufficiently sturdy.

THE PATIO VERSION: The most successful version of an aboveground pond starts with one of the smaller, pre-formed liners. You probably need to fit it into a box of some kind. Some gardeners build a housing of bricks around the shape; a sturdy wooden box will also do the trick. Make the housing wider, longer, and deeper if you want to add insulation (2-inch-thick plastic foam insulation is fine) or additional landscape elements. In any event, as a finishing touch, you'll want to top off the housing with a cap that juts out over the liner's rim and hides it from view. This can be the same material (e.g. wood) or even some pretty tiles.

THE YARD VERSION: This sort is often larger than the little patio version, simply because there's more space for it. Still, the plants and creatures in

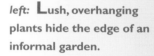

left: **L**ush, overhanging plants hide the edge of an informal garden.

right: **C**arefully positioned, and securely anchored, rocks help make a water feature look natural and informal.

Here is an example of a strong and sturdy raised pool.

WATER-ONLY DISPLAYS

Where light is limited, or you just want a reflecting pool or simply a splashy fountain, your "water garden" may turn out to contain water only. (Note that very agitated or "busy" water is not very welcoming to waterlilies and some other aquatic plants, which prosper in still water. Fish, however, may appreciate the aeration.) The way you tuck it into its surroundings and/or landscape around it can make it look like it belongs and make that part of your garden very special indeed. For a successful display:

- Keep the pool or catch basin in scale with its surroundings.

- A sheltered location is often best. It's practical—the wind won't ruffle the water or toss a fountain's spray about. And it's prettier—you can create a sense of tranquility.

- A little shade is desirable. While algae prospers in open water in full sun, it is less likely to gain a foothold in less light. Also, open pools (particularly if they're not very deep) can really heat up in hot sun, another condition algae likes.

- Consider blue or black water dyes. These are not a good idea in fish pools (because you won't be able to see the fish, not because the dyes are harmful), but a water-only pool can benefit. The dyes darken the water, depriving it of the light algae needs to grow. You get an inky, mirror-like surface.

A reflecting pool is perfect for this setting, which already has enough "plant activity."

- Enhance the display with statuary, other ornaments, or some overhanging plants—ferns or hostas are especially pretty.

such a pool ought to be removed each fall. And whether made of concrete, fiberglass, or plastic, empty or full, an aboveground pool will be vulnerable to structural damage such as buckling or cracking. So this sort of aboveground pool is best attempted in mild climates only.

That said, aboveground pools can be dramatic and handsome additions to a landscape. Your best bet is to start with a high-quality preformed liner and put a wall around it—for support, of course, but also to make it look nicer and to protect it from the sun's rays, which can cause the plastic to become brittle over time.

Waterfalls and Streams

A cascading waterfall or gurgling stream may be your dream, and if your property is not blessed with a natural one, it is indeed possible to install one. Done with care and attention to detail, the end result can look quite natural and provide many years of delight to both your eyes and ears.

An existing slope on your property is good luck, but even then, tinkering will be required to fit this sort of water feature into its surroundings. If the site you have in mind is relatively flat, a waterfall or tumbling stream can still be installed, but of course you'll need to change the grade by importing a base of soil and/or rocks.

If you have something ambitious in mind, assess the intended site with the help of a professional, educate yourself on what is involved, and be willing to pay for expert help. You want it to be done right, so it's a pleasure and not a heartache, so it brings the music of moving water to your property and operates like it should.

Big or small, hold fast to your vision, bear up under the time-consuming, backbreaking work (or be patient with the contractors), and one day, the water will flow and it will have all been worth it!

Straight lines confer a formal feel.

Bubblers add soothing sounds as well as a refreshing sight in a small, shady space.

This backyard waterfall is made of concrete and stones.

WATERFALL ADVICE:

■ Kits are the easiest to install and take the work of calculations off your hands. These include a pre-formed plastic run—complete with occasional small basins, if you like—and end with a lip that fits onto a pre-formed pond (so you can buy them as a set). And waterfall kits either come with or recommend a specific size/capacity pump and the tubing necessary for routing the flow.

■ If you choose a free-form waterfall, there's no need to acquire a very long piece of flexible liner. You can cut shorter pieces for ease of installation—just overlap each one by at least a foot, and plan to work from the bottom to the top of the run.

■ Make sure the basin or basins are level and secure because when the water is flowing, they can overflow to the sides or dislodge if they're not level and firmly in place.

■ When installing tubing from the pump, set it up with as few bends or angles as possible because these restrict or slow down the flow of the water.

■ Ideally, run your outlet tube alongside your watercourse, as close as you can get it. (You can hide it from view with mulch and/or lush plantings.) This way, you can gain access to it if there is ever a problem, such as a clog.

■ To make the final installation look more realistic and to hide the liner, incorporate plenty of real stones and some plants along the sides. Mortaring the stones in place will prevent slippage.

STREAM SAVVY:

■ Position the streambed so the actual watercourse is below ground level. You may bank the edges.

■ The water should be level (from side-to-side) as it runs through the system (even if one bank is steeper than the other).

■ Install a larger stream in sections. Pre-formed plastic (polyethylene) and fiberglass watercourses that include the necessary grade changes are available.

TOOLS AND SUPPLIES CHECKLIST FOR STREAMS

Here's what you need:

- A pump that can handle the job, complete with tubing and an electrical cord to route and power its work.
- A GFCI (or GFI), a "ground fault circuit interrupter" or "ground fault interrupter," an extension-cord style device that automatically shuts off power when it detects a leak in the electrical current (thus preventing shock).
- Plastic liner (either sheeting or pre-formed).
- Sharp-edged, durable shovels, or, for large projects, earth-moving equipment.
- A carpenter's level and boards, or a laser level.
- Rocks and stones, for the sides as well as the bed.

■ Vary the width along the course, and create occasional basins.

■ Get professional help when calculating the water volume and choosing the right pump for the job.

■ Intersperse rocks. This varies the flow, looks natural, and increases water sounds. Create ripples in shallower water with large pebbles, or add submerged rocks to deeper water. Rocks on the banks or breaking the water surface are also worthwhile touches.

■ Create a several-inch overflow area on both sides of the stream to handle flooding from heavy rains.

■ In spring and fall, especially, monitor your stream and remove excessive debris that has fallen from nearby plants or overhead trees so the water can flow freely.

■ Try hard to prevent potential leaks during set-up, and check your waterfall for leaks after installation. Typical trouble spots are under rocks, within the liner (if damaged), and over edges.

Fountains

No doubt about it, a fountain brings wonderful focus and excitement to any garden.

The splish-splash it creates is enticing and often soothing as well, drawing visitors. It may even distract from street noise, but just as the size of the feature ought to be in scale with its surroundings, so should the sound—you don't want Niagara Falls on a small patio!

There are so many choices in terms of style, size, and sound that you might just want to go shopping

If your yard has enough room, you can have a stream and a waterfall.

before you make up your mind where your fountain will go. Water-garden centers, home and garden centers, and mail-order suppliers offer an amazing range of options. For perhaps more stylish or customized fountains, search on the Internet for artists who specialize in such creations or prowl arts-and-crafts shows. The pump and tubing generally come with the fountain, so you don't have to worry about capacity and power calculations.

Alternatively, you can purchase an urn, bowl, or kettle that catches your fancy and have a professional turn it into a fountain feature for you by rigging the necessary tubing and pump.

Whatever you buy, you want it to be durable and watertight. These days, resins that look like cement but don't crack or leak as easily have surpassed cement fountains. Cast concrete ones can be found, too, as well as ceramic and other materials.

HOW THEY WORK: A small, submerged pump circulates water up through plastic tubing into the fountain, which returns it to a catch basin. From there, it is pumped back up through the tubing.

The right fountain brings a lot of style and enchantment.

MAINTAINING YOUR FOUNTAIN

- Keep an eye on the water level and top off the fountain with a little extra water on windy or hot days if evaporation is lowering it.

- Keep the water clear of debris, as leaves and other plant litter can clog the tubing and fountain nozzle.

- If your water is "hard" or leaves mineral deposits, this can clog your fountain over time. You can get chemicals from water-garden suppliers to treat this condition. Alternatively, use distilled (purified) water.

- Turn off the fountain if you are going to be away for an extended period—you wouldn't want a clogging problem to occur when nobody is around to clear it.

- If you have freezing winters, you need to drain the fountain completely in the fall, cover it, and store the hardware indoors.

- Periodically, screens and nozzles must be cleaned out—check them often, especially if water flow seems decreased, and/or follow the maintenance schedule and directions from the manufacturer.

SETTING UP: It is very important that a fountain, no matter how small or large, is set up on a level surface. Patios, terraces, and decks ought to be no problem, but if you're tucking a fountain into a garden bed, you might want to lay down pavers or a concrete slab to provide stability and support (check it for levelness and wiggle it and adjust the soil). Be sure to pack the soil well once it's leveled.

HIDING THE HARDWARE: The electrical cable that powers the pump can be hidden in the base of some fountains; otherwise, route it out over the side and away. A grounded outlet should be nearby, and you'll want to camouflage the cord, probably with some plants.

SPRAY OPTIONS: Spray height and shape (from a gentle, misty fan to a towering spurt) is determined not only by the power of the pump but by the nozzle on the fountain's head. Often the same fountain can be fitted with a variety of nozzles, so examine your options and find something you like.

FOUNTAINS WITH PLANTS AND FISH: While a number of water plants, notably marginals and some floaters, are fine with moving water, waterlilies and lotuses are not! So either site the fountain at one end of your larger planted water garden, choose a very slow-drip or slow-flow fountain . . . or don't have one in the pool at all. As for fish, they appreciate the way sprinkling water keeps the pool water aerated (low oxygen levels are a leading cause of fish death). Run the fountain all night on hot summer nights, when the fish will especially need that agitation (because water plants are not releasing oxygen into the water at night).

FOUNTAINS WITH NO PLANTS OR FISH: Inhibit algae growth by treating the water with some sort of clarifier. You can get such products from the place where you bought the fountain or from any water-garden supplier. (Alternatively, a bit of bleach or vinegar may do the trick.)

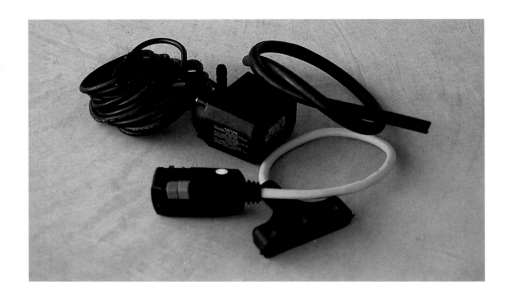

Pumps and Filters

Unless you are an accomplished do-it-yourselfer, your best bet is to seek professional advice about pumps and filters for your water garden. Talk with a specialist or a landscaper who installs water features or call a mail-order supplier and discuss your options. Their expertise will be invaluable. You may also decide to hire someone to do the installation for you. That said, you should still be an educated consumer.

A pump's job is to recirculate water in your pond or to power a filter, fountain, stream, or waterfall. You need to make sure that the equipment is a match for the job or you'll burn out the motor—again, seek expert advice here. There are always performance charts on the packages (and in the website or catalog descriptions), if you want to study them—the basic gist is how many gallons per hour they can handle. "Head" or "lift" refers to the various heights above the pump that it can lift water. It's a good idea to estimate conservatively, so the pump can manage the job you're asking of it without being maxed out.

There are two kinds of pumps: submersible and external. The submersible, or sunken ones, are best in small pools, where they sit out of sight near the bottom, quietly keeping the water moving. They do have to be removed and cleaned periodically. To make this easier, you can set the pump in a small mesh container or laundry basket and haul the entire thing out from time to time for cleaning; these will capture much of the plant debris and leaves before they can get to the pump and cause damage.

To keep the pump out of any muck on the bottom of the pond, set it on bricks, a cinder block, or overturned clay pot. Remember to check the pump occasionally to be sure it is functioning properly and to clean off any filter screens.

External or out-of-water pumps, on the other hand, can handle bigger jobs—large pools, a series of pools, or pools with waterfall or stream features. But you will probably want to find a way to hide them from view even as they sit close by your water feature, perhaps behind a barrier or lush plant. Just be sure it's a safe spot, where it can't be knocked over and is not accessible to curious children. And be warned: These pumps can be rather noisy, although manufacturers are working to minimize this.

Installation can also be tricky or risky for a novice. Pumps require electricity, which involves a cable (that you can hopefully disguise or bury on its way to the nearest outlet) and a GFCI outlet for safety. Speaking of the nearest outlet, it's also advisable for the outlet to have its own circuit so it doesn't interfere with other household appliances and so you can easily trip the breaker if there's ever a problem. Again, these various and important requirements are probably best handled for you by a professional electrician.

Filters, on the other hand, are simple contraptions, intended to protect the pump and improve water quality. Mechanical ones have mesh or foam screens that need to be rinsed off often, even daily or weekly during the height of summer. They are good for trapping algae and larger pool debris. Select a filter that is appropriate for your water feature; one with a very fine mesh will clog easily if your pond has a lot of algae and fine particles in it, requiring frequent cleaning and the likelihood of ruining the pump by burning it out.

If you have fish, they generate waste, which means your water garden will need more filtration and a bigger system. A

Unless you are an accomplished do-it-yourselfer, your best bet is to seek professional advice about pumps and filters for your water garden.

CAN'T MISS TIP:

CLEANER STILL

If you have koi, large fish that produce a lot of waste, you may also want to invest in a UV clarifier. These use ultraviolet light to sterilize water as it enters your pump; purified water is then pumped back into the pool.

biological filter allows your pool to cope. Basically, it uses gravel and beneficial bacteria to clean the water and convert fish waste (primarily ammonia) into nitrate, boosting water health for the fish as well as the plant residents. Biological filters generally sit outside, but close to, the pool, above the water level (you can use plants, potted or otherwise, to hide the device from view if you don't want to look at it). They require less frequent cleaning because they work at a slower pace than mechanical filters; you can rinse them every few weeks or once a month. Be sure to use pond water for rinsing, though, not tap water, which will kill the bacteria colonies that you want.

Lighting a Water Garden

Increase the hours your water garden can be enjoyed—and give an entirely different perspective—by investing in lighting. In particular, if you grow night-blooming tropical waterlilies, you will want to enjoy them after the sun goes down.

This could be as simple as ordinary floodlights strategically installed close by in your yard. Or you could enjoy the drama of underwater lighting

Saavy positioning of garden lighting brings drama to your water garden at night.

right in your pond or fountain. Some pond kits already come with such lighting features.

All this, of course, is in addition to lights you may need to install in your garden for safety reasons, such as bulbs under the rails of a pond bridge or path-side lights. It's possible to rig all the wiring together, at the same time.

In any event, as with the other water-garden elements that require electrical wiring (and, always, please, a GFCI device for safety), installation is best left to a professional. Be sure to hire someone whose work you have seen and admired, who comes recommended, and who is licensed and insured. A good contractor will also have tricks up his sleeve for disguising or hiding the fixtures and wiring from view. In any event, get an estimate on the work beforehand so there are no surprises!

Here are some of your many dramatic options:

■ BACKGROUND LIGHTING: the lights illuminate nearby tall trees, walls, or fences.

■ SPOTLIGHTING: when a floodlight is aimed at a specific spot or surface.

■ UPLIGHTING: when the lighting is down low and aims upward; a great way to highlight garden trees near your water garden or a waterfall or impressive plant with a vertical growth habit.

■ DOWNLIGHTING: lighting that is installed up high in a tree or on a roof, wall, or fence, so that items below are illuminated—your pond's surface, or a waterfall, for instance.

■ MOONLIGHTING: when a series of lights are erected up high to filter down through tree branches and foliage, creating complex shadows on the water garden and adjacent landscaping below.

■ SILHOUETTING: when you install a strong light behind a large plant or object, causing it to stand out.

■ GRAZING: the light beam should rake across the water's surface . . . thus it needs to be mounted low and strategically for best impact.

■ UNDERWATER LIGHTING: the light fixture is under the water surface, strategically placed to illuminate your plants and other water-garden features from below. These should be installed at the time that the pool is put in and before the water is added, of course; some liner kits come with the necessary hardware, wiring, and instructions.

CAN'T MISS TIP:

SOFTER LIGHT IS BETTER

You don't want glare, especially around water. A softer effect, like moonlight, is much more desirable. So work with your electrician or contractor not only on the position of individual lights but on the strength and even the color of the illumination. (Soft white or yellow is popular, but blue or green lights can be enchanting.)

Plants, Fish, and More

Like any other new garden area, a water garden has the potential to hold all kinds of fabulous plants, including many that may be new to you. Some have gorgeous flowers, some have attractive, variegated, or intriguing foliage, and some have both—so you have plenty of appealing choices. You will learn more about the various kinds of plants in this chapter, and in individual detail in the Plant Directory, but here's a quick overview.

Outright aquatic/water-loving plants are always an obvious choice—waterlilies as well as small-sized (and correspondingly smaller-flowered) plants that float on the water's surface. There are also lots of plants that either tolerate or actually thrive on being immersed a few inches deep. These are best potted and set on a side shelf inside your water garden or elevated on some sort of platform so they're not too deep under the water. Though commonly referred to as "marginals," because they are naturals for the margins of a water display, they are also sometimes called "bog plants." A lot of irises meet this description, and cattails, of course, but there are plenty of others of similar form and size that you might like.

And last but not least are plants that live mainly submerged below the water's surface. They are there less for their good looks (though some are perfectly attractive) than for practical reasons of contributing oxygen and providing some shelter and spawning areas for fish.

Speaking of fish, they are optional in a water garden, but they certainly add to the viewing pleasure. Smaller ones, such as common goldfish, are nice to have because they eat mosquito larvae. Bigger ones, especially the ornamental carp known as koi, are very beautiful and also interactive—they can be trained to eat small fish snacks out of your outstretched hand; they are actually considered pets by some enthusiasts. There's information about fish in this chapter as well, so you can decide whether you want to add some.

It's also a nice touch to include some décor in your display. You might like to have a ceramic frog perched on the edge, or an Aquarius statue, or any number of other accents that add fun and style.

But before you plunge in and start adding anything to your new water garden, let's pause and consider what is important, not only for your display's good looks but also for its health.

Simplicity is often best. Unless you've put in a large, ambitious pond, your space is limited. This is a bit like installing a new flowerbed, in the sense that although you know there are dozens of great plants you might wish to grow, the reality is you need to rein yourself in. Adding too many plants—no matter how attractive they may be—ends up looking like a hodgepodge, and the overcrowding isn't good for them and can cause you extra mainte-

The most successful water gardens have a combination of horizontal plants, like waterlilies, and spiky, vertical growers.

nance. So resolve to try a few beauties this year. You can always refine your displays and try different ones next year!

Please note that plants mentioned in the following pages are individually pictured and described in more detail in Chapter 4, along with similar choices. When you're ready, thumb through that chapter and start making your shopping list.

Design Made Easy

Water gardens are wonderfully versatile. Depending on the plants you choose to put in the water and the ones you choose to gather around the sides, totally different moods and effects are possible. Still water may be adorned with waterlilies and water-loving accent or marginal/bog plants (plus certain other plants not as visible at first glance but still important to the display's success), while moving water can splash its merry way past clumps of lush arrowhead plants and handsome cattails.

Contrasting Horizontal and Vertical

In any garden, a balance of horizontal and vertical elements keeps things interesting—it moves the eye around, it invites exploration. A water feature's role can go either way, depending on how you site it and what you put into it (plant-wise as well as what sorts of decorative accents you include). True, the plane of the water is flat and horizontal, but add upright-growing potted plants or a fountain, and you've got vertical interest. Let's examine the possibilities. As you read and study the photographs, try to think what you would like and would look best in the setting you've chosen for your water feature.

HORIZONTAL WATER GARDENS: If your yard features trees, especially tall or columnar ones, or other upright plants such as ornamental grasses, or if the water feature has been sited near a vertical non-plant feature such as an arbor, gazebo, or wall, the horizontal water surface naturally and automatically offsets these elements. In such a case, your best bet may be to emphasize the pond's flat surface. You can:

■ let it be a reflecting pool.
■ only put low lying, flatter, surface-growing plants in the pool.

Vertical elements behind a water garden help bring the eye to it by framing it.

The stones in this water garden add vertical interest.

■ use only a handful of vertical-growing marginals, near the edges of the pool, where they will set up a modest echo of their surroundings.

VERTICAL WATER GARDENS: Draw every garden visitor to your pond or container garden with a dramatic approach to its landscaping that highlights its presence and its contents. Go up by filling it with vertical elements. To do this:

■ include plants, mainly marginals, that have a strong vertical growth habit. This includes everything from cattails to ornamental grasses to papyrus to taro to umbrella palm, just to name a few common possibilities.

■ add a tall, non-plant accent such as statuary.

■ put in a fountain whose spray spurts upward.

Color in the Water Garden

Working with color in a pond or other water feature is not essentially different from dealing with it in other parts of your garden. Many of the same principles apply; the information given below is tailored to water plants, which offer a rainbow of choices. But remember, green is a color, too.

Please note: Assuming you want waterlilies—arguably the star attraction of many water displays—and have the six or so hours of sun per day that allows them to thrive, it is likely they will become your dominant plant. It isn't just their size and attention-grabbing form; well-grown waterlilies also have the potential to remain in bloom for months. So our discussion of color is dominated by them. If your water garden is not large, you will find yourself

CAN'T MISS TIP:

USE CONTRAST WITHIN A DISPLAY

With the water garden itself as the canvas, it is common to mix and match horizontally growing plants with tall, slender ones. Done sparingly, the display is interesting and attractive. Overdone, however, and the show is just "too busy," causing the eye to dart around, unable to come to rest on any one plant. Be careful, too, not to block shorter plants from view by crowding the sides of the pool (this is a common mistake when you are overzealous with lining marginal plants along your pond's side shelves). Strike a balance within the water feature between the two types of plants—vertical and horizontal— and again, remember that less is usually better. Simplicity is beautiful.

The pale blue 'Dauben' flower glows against the dark leaves.

shopping for waterlilies by color from the outset and perhaps only choosing one or a handful. So it's common for waterlily bloom color to set your color theme.

That said, there are of course plenty of other worthy plants that you can grow and that will contribute to the color show. Smaller plants can share the spotlight if you use that old landscaper's trick of grouping them; for instance, a cluster of three blue-flowered marginals can be a fair match for one yellow-blooming waterlily. Or a substitute, for that matter. In any event, as you start to survey your choices, begin by considering your setting, looking at such aspects as the background scenery and the amount of sun.

If your in-ground garden is already a riot of color:

■ let your water garden be an oasis of peaceful green, providing a rest for the eyes.

■ grow some of the many water plants that sport handsome foliage, such as cannas, taros, and irises (with or without variegated spears).

If your water feature does not get lots of sun:

■ grow a variety of foliage textures, shapes, and shades of green; this "layered effect" can be quite gorgeous and fascinating.

■ use variegated-leaved plants specifically for their foliage; this includes irises, certain ornamental grasses, sweet flag, and houttuynia.

■ grow shade-tolerant plants.

The backdrop for your water garden might be predominantly green, whether from lawn or shrubbery or both. Depending on where you place the water feature, that adjacent and surrounding green may be a factor in your color choices in and by the water. Significant coverage of the water surface by lilypads and floating green foliage also causes the color green to dominate. This is your opportunity to have fun with color in the water garden.

If there is a lot of green and your water feature gets plentiful sun, you will find that:

■ contrasting colors such as bright yellow and white are sure to stand out.

■ darker hues such as purple and red will stand out better if grown alongside some white or yellow partners.

■ white, cream, or neutral-hued statuary are dramatic additions.

■ echoing an in-pond color with a similar color on the banks or at least nearby really helps make a stronger statement (for instance, blue waterlilies in the pool with blue irises or hydrangea growing in the ground nearby).

Realize that the water surface is a neutral canvas, allowing for many possibilities. This is why so many handsome color combinations are possible in a water garden. Here are some examples to use for inspiration.

DYNAMIC DUOS: Two-color displays are a great idea for smaller water features and containers; they deliver a lot of punch. Here are just a few possibilities:

■ PINK AND PURPLE: pink tropical waterlily (such as 'Evelyn Randig') with blue pickerel rush.

■ BLUE AND YELLOW: blue tropical waterlily (such as dwarf 'Dauben' or 'Teri Dunn') with yellow water poppy.

■ RED AND YELLOW: red-leaved taro with golden club; red-flowered and yellow-flowered cannas together.

■ PEACH AND BLUE: hardy peach waterlily (such as 'Peaches and Cream' or 'Comanche') with blue water hyacinth.

WINNING PRIMARIES: Seek out red, yellow, and as true a blue as you can get, then put them together in the same display to make a bold impression. Some proven combinations include:

■ hardy waterlily red (such as 'James Brydon' or 'Escarboucle'), hardy waterlily yellow (such as 'Chromatella'), tropical waterlily blue (such as 'Tina' or 'Panama Pacific').

Water gardens are pretty in pastels.

CAN'T MISS TIP:

NIGHT BLOOMERS

Did you know that some waterlilies, tropical ones, are at their peak during the evening hours? These glorious flowers rise high above the water surface, open in late afternoon, and often remain so into the following morning. Thus they are ideal for busy people who are away at work or school all day! Growing these will entice you to go into the yard in the evening hours to relax near the display—a glorious way to unwind and reconnect with nature.

A monochromatic design that flows through the water and onto the banks can be very striking—and soothing to behold.

■ red cardinal flower, yellow water poppy, blue flag iris.

■ red-flowered canna, yellow tropical waterlily (such as 'St. Louis Gold'), blue pickerel rush.

PRETTY PASTELS: When your water garden is a place of refuge or retreat, softer colors are often the ideal choice. Lighter colors mix well with one another, and the whole becomes greater than the sum of its parts. Note also that adding a soothing glow of white is always welcome.

■ pink, purple, and white: pink tropical waterlily (such as 'Queen of Siam' or 'General Pershing'), blue-purple tropical waterlily (such as 'Rhonda Kay' or 'Panama Pacific'), white lizard's tail.

■ soft yellow, lavender, white: yellow floating heart, lavender iris, white-flowered arrowhead.

■ pink, soft yellow, pale purple: pink hardy waterlily (such as 'Mayla' or 'Colorado'), yellow canna, purple iris.

SUNRISE, SUNSET: A pond dedicated to hues of pink, orange, and yellow is lovely indeed. There are a few waterlilies, prosaically known as "changeables," whose blossoms actually run through all three of these colors, generally starting out lighter and gradually deepening as the days go by. Some lotuses also have this quality. At least one of these is worth building this theme around.

■ changeable hardy waterlily (such as 'Peaches and Cream' or 'Sioux'), pink canna, yellow water poppy.

■ changeable hardy waterlily (such as 'Comanche'), houttuynia (which has pink-splashed, heart-shaped leaves).

■ yellow tropical waterlily (such as 'St. Louis Gold'), multicolored tropical waterlily (such as 'Albert Greenberg'), pink tropical waterlily (such as 'Texas Shell Pink' or 'Evelyn Randig').

■ lotus (rosy 'Mrs. Perry D. Slocum' or 'Momo Botan'), yellow hardy waterlily (such as 'Joey Tomocik').

MONOCHROMATIC SHOWS: Single-color displays are a great idea when your surrounding garden is already busy with color and you want to help your pool stand out. They are also a wise tactic when your overall landscaping is formal or simple, and you want your new addition, the water garden, to harmonize with its surroundings.

Group different shades of the same color in a display. For example, try light and dark purple together, or soft and bright yellow. Or all white, a favorite approach for those who enjoy their water garden in the evening hours when white flowers really glow. (Two excellent night-blooming white waterlilies, both tropicals, are 'Trudy Slocum' and 'Wood's White Knight'.)

Here are some combination ideas:

- WHITE: white tropical waterlily (such as 'Josephine' or 'Marian Strawn'), lizard's tail, white water snowflake.
- BLUE: blue tropical waterlily (such as 'Tina' or 'Dauben'), pickerel rush, blue iris.
- PURPLE: purple tropical waterlily (such as 'Panama Pacific') with 'Black Magic' taro.

YELLOW AS AN ACCENT: Most waterlilies have yellow centers (a flush of bright, prominent stamens). Placing an all-yellow waterlily next to one with, say, purple petals and a yellow interior, makes for an especially dramatic display. (A classic example: yellow 'St. Louis Gold' alongside purple 'Panama Pacific'.) For a variation on this effect, grow yellow-blooming marginals and floaters. (For example, water poppies have boldly shaped, buttery yellow flowers in enough profusion to call out the yellow in their neighbors.)

CAN'T MISS
TIP:

A FEW GOOD COLOR "TRICKS"

Go for the bold: Create some sizzling scenes by grouping flowers (and foliage—some cannas that thrive in water gardens have bright-striped leaves) in shades of sunny yellow, bright red, and fiery orange. Magenta and royal purple make daring accents in this context.

A little jolt: Widen a display's color range slightly to punch up interest—add a little blue to a purple composition, a little peach to a yellow, and so forth.

Depth perception: Calming, cooler cools and pastels seem to recede, while exciting warmer colors appear to advance or look closer.

Working with Texture and Foliage

You may have noticed that savvy use of texture is "all the rage" these days in perennial gardens, public parks, and even container-garden displays. Water gardeners can certainly have fun and employ their creativity by tapping into this gardening trend.

Contrasting foliage shapes and colors make your water display more interesting.

LILYPAD COLORS

Variegated lilypads can be as exciting as their flowers.

Oftentimes, young lilypads are maroon or bronze when small and give over to shades of green as they mature. But for a time, this juvenile color is a nice contrast to their flowers, particularly red, maroon, or purple-hued waterlilies.

And some lilypads are splashed and dotted with colors and remain that way, usually red, maroon, purple, even pink, and also sometimes yellow or cream. Their undersides may also be brown, red, or purple. This more durable, longer-lasting color contribution is natural and sometimes quite dramatic in contrast to waterlily flowers. A clever water gardener might also find ways to echo and thus emphasize the presence of this coloration in their choices of marginals and floaters. (These lilypads are also a boon to water gardens that receive less sun because, even though the flowering is reduced in less sun, the plants are still worth growing for the attractive color they provide!) Possibilities include:

- the purple-splashed leaves of the tropical waterlily 'Albert Greenberg' alongside any purple-flowered Japanese iris, in shallow water or on the edges of your water garden.

- the olive-green leaves of a waterlily (such as the hardy 'Arc-en-Ciel') are liberally marked with cream, pink, yellow, and even red; pair it with the rosy-pink flowers of flowering rush (*Butomus umbellatus*) or red- or pink-flowered astilbes on the banks of your pool.

- bogbean (*Menyanthes trifoliata*) has tiny white flowers that are pink in bud; the spikes are a flurry of pink and white. This marginal or floater thus looks nice with any purple or pink-splashed lilypad.

Professional garden designers get a lot of unexpected and delightful beauty by using different plant forms—and you can, too. Work texture and foliage to your advantage in your water garden when:

- there is limited space and you want to create the illusion of depth.
- the water feature is in a shady location.
- you want low-maintenance, season-long drama.
- there are objects or views you wish to disguise or hide.
- you enjoy seeing a variety of foliage types growing together.
- you want your display to be always interesting, even when plants are not in bloom.

FINE/DELICATE: papyrus, umbrella palm, floating heart, duckweed, parrot's feather, ferns.

MEDIUM: ornamental grasses, cattails, iris, arrowhead, water hyacinth.

BOLD: all waterlilies (hardy and tropical), all lotus, canna, taro, thalia.

PUTTING IT ALL TOGETHER: Mixing textures is an art, and it's also a matter of personal taste. Here are some tips to get you started.

1. Avoid massing too much of one plant. It's okay to favor one over another, but tuck in some contrasting "punctuation" if you can from a few different-textured plants.
2. Guard against any scene becoming too busy. Keep it simple.
3. Work with foliage color. If you find two or more plants of the same leaf color, but of different textures, let them be near one another in your pond. Or try sharp contrast, as when very dark green glossy leaves are adjacent to chartreuse or yellow-tinged foliage.
4. Layer plants in the pond (floating, mid-height, tall) for interest. Shrubs, vines, even small trees near a pool add additional levels.
5. When a combination works, be willing to maintain it. This may mean occasional clipping or pruning, or even tearing out plants that spread beyond their appointed spot.

Decorative Touches

After you've settled on the plants you'd like to grow in your water garden, consider adding a bit of flair with an ornament, statue, or other decorative

THE TROPICAL LOOK

Although a hot, humid climate nurtures a tropical-themed water garden, you still can achieve the look even in cooler climates.

- **Go lush:** Include plenty of foliage plants, particularly large-leaved or coarse-textured ones. Landscape the side of the pond with more of the same.

- **Use bright, bold colors:** Employ waterlilies and marginals in deep, decisive hues—no pastels need apply!

- **Add accents:** Include any object, sculpture, or statue that has a Central American, African, Caribbean, or Indian origin or look.

- **Running water:** This is an informal type of garden, so the source can be a trickling stream, running waterfall, or lively fountain.

Large-leaved tropical marginals, like this taro, make for a lush look.

THE ASIAN LOOK

Always a popular design influence on water gardens! Get ideas and inspiration by thumbing through magazines or books that have plenty of photographs of Asian-influenced gardens, even if you don't specifically see water features in their pages.

- Set it up in a secluded or somewhat hidden corner of your yard.

- Keep the display uncluttered.

- Grow a lotus plant, even if your water isn't warm enough or the spot isn't sunny enough for it to bloom—the leaves are gorgeous in their own right.

- Palm-like plants, in moderation, are a must, both in the pond and adjacent.

- Add appropriate accents, such as Japanese lanterns, Asian-influenced statuary, or a small bridge.

- If there is moving water, let it be subtle, such as a gentle trickle into a shallow basin. (Some suppliers offer attractive, small bamboo-cane water spouts.)

- Add goldfish or koi. (For more on fish, please see page 62.)

An Asian look is always popular and attractive.

element. Water features really seem to welcome a little something extra because it often helps integrate them into their surroundings. A frog or heron made of stone, say, or a ceramic turtle, fits in nicely and gives lots of personality and charm.

MATERIALS: Like anything else, you get what you pay for! Quality water-garden ornaments are handsome, well crafted, outdoor-appropriate, and durable. They are available in everything from cement to terra-cotta to carved stone to resin that looks like stone. Or you can go for an object made of iron, brass, bronze, cast aluminum, or even wood. If it will be in contact with the water, ask how it will wear over time and figure out whether you need a supplemental support for its base. It will likely get plenty of sun, so find out whether it is expected to fade or gain a green patina (either of which might be okay with you) or flake (which might not!). If your winters are freezing, you need to know if it can be left outside or needs to be brought into the garage or basement every fall. And finally, if it's a substantial or expen-

This heron sculpture will cause less damage to your water garden than a real one would.

sive piece of work, find out about a warranty and read the fine print about exposure to the elements.

PLACEMENT: The item should enhance your display, not clutter it or detract from it. In color, size, and height, it should be clearly visible and not out of scale. So if it's going into the pond, you might site it to one side or one end, in a spot where there are fewer plants, so it can stand out. If you perch your decorative object on the side, be sure it's secure, that is, not vulnerable to being knocked over, or knocked into the water, either by a clumsy visitor or by a stiff breeze.

ORNAMENTAL WATER FEATURES: Fountains that add to the water show, however minimal, are a common and very appealing choice. There are fish and dolphins that send a thin, arching stream of water into the pool and birds and frogs and other small creatures that "spit" water a short distance (these ornaments are literally called "spitters"). There are water cherub and Aquarius figurine fountains that pour water from an urn. And so on. If small, the water they emit should not unduly disturb plants that prefer still water, like many waterlilies. However, they do require—and generally come with—small pumps and electrical cords to power the display. If you are at all daunted about installing a fountain that requires electrical power near water, by all means call a qualified electrician—better safe than sorry. (And don't forget a GFCI must be included with all electrical cords.)

"Spitter" fountains, like this frog, will not stir up the water and thus are appropriate with waterlilies.

CAN'T MISS TIP:

DÉCOR SHOPPING

Your best bet is any garden center or catalog that specializes in supplies for water gardening—there, you are sure to find a broad selection. Plus, you can be certain the ornament, statue, or fountain is made from an appropriate material (and comes with all the right hardware). Alternatively, general garden-supply sources may have some nice items, or you can prowl flea markets and yard sales for unique objects. If you're seeking something really special, look in art studios, craft marts, arts-and-crafts shows, art galleries, and ceramics studios. Just bear in mind the "exposure to the elements" issues!

Establishing Ecological Balance

There's a bit more to stocking a water garden than just picking out appealing plants and pretty fish. When you're a beginner, you soon discover that there are too many wonderful plants and too little pool! While the temptation is great to put in all sorts of gorgeous waterlilies, plus an assortment of stately marginals and some pretty floating plants, alas, it's just not realistic. As for fish, it's never a good idea to buy some without knowing what the pool can support (more on that later).

Just as with a new flower border or vegetable garden at the beginning of the growing season, a big assortment looks like it will fit at first. But plants grow. And water plants really grow, some so eagerly that in a matter of weeks they become crowded and need to be thinned. They jockey for light and space, flower less or stop blooming altogether, and leaves can begin to die back. Crowded waterlilies will rear their lilypads up out of the water in a desperate bid for space ("pyramiding") that is neither good for them nor attractive. If you don't intervene, the pool becomes an overgrown tangle. So restraint is in order!

The fact is, all garden pools can and should achieve the desirable state known as "balance," the stable point where plants and creatures support one another. This happens perhaps more easily and with more complexity in the wild, but it is attainable in the contained and finite environment of a home water garden, too.

Here's how it works. Oxygen produced by the plants is consumed by animal life, which in turn provides carbon dioxide for the plants. This is the same cycle that occurs on a vast scale in the natural world around us, and it is a cycle that must establish and sustain itself in the little world of your

FLOATING DÉCOR

One pool-decorating idea that has become more popular in recent years is launching a floating object. Check out what water-garden suppliers have to offer and see what might appeal to you. Options include orbs, lights, and "floating islands" that can hold a plant or two.

water garden. Additionally, over time (or prompted by a "starter"), beneficial bacteria will become established in your pool. Their role is to convert plant and animal wastes into non-toxic compounds, which in turn are used by the plants.

Two-thirds Coverage

Both research and experience have taught water gardeners that a successful home pool has about two-thirds of its surface covered with plants, and one-third exposed or open. When two-thirds of the water surface is shielded by plant growth, three things happen:

- A well-covered pool resists algae problems. This is because algae need lots of sunlight to grow and gain a foothold. Shade thwarts algae.
- Pond creatures can thrive in a safe sanctuary. If a predatory bird should stop by, they can hide under the foliage of floating plants. The sheltering foliage also can discourage marauding raccoons, muskrats, and the like.
- The pond water is cooler than water that is open and exposed to the hot sun. This becomes more important if your summers are quite hot.

You may be wondering, why not full coverage? But a water feature literally choked with plants is not healthy (no sun gets in, air/oxygen does not circulate), plus you deprive yourself of one of water gardening's greatest pleasures, viewing reflections in the water. Indeed, an overplanted pond hardly looks like a pond . . . it ends up looking more like a neglected, overgrown bog.

Setting Up . . . Then Waiting

Bearing the two-thirds coverage rule in mind, then, you the gardener can and must exert control at the outset. Do this by choosing the right number of plants (based on their mature size, of course, not the size they are when you first get them).

After that, you must stand back and let the pool do the rest, intervening only when the plants need a bit of trimming back. A healthy pool—one "in balance"—has a sustainable number of plants, fish, and perhaps other creatures, and, actually, a slight tinge of amber or green algae.

Your plants should cover two-thirds of your pool surface for optimum health.

How long should you wait for balance to occur? This depends on several factors, including your climate/the weather, the time of year, and the intervals at which you add plants and fish . . . but you can reasonably expect a moderately sized garden pond to reach a desirable state of equilibrium after six or more weeks.

How long can you expect your pool to stay in balance? Assuming you care for it and the contents properly, it can remain in balance indefinitely.

Finding Out What Your Pond Can Hold

A home water garden is a finite environment. So, you should be able to determine how many plants and other residents it can hold while remaining in good health. This doesn't take a lot of sophisticated math, but you should figure out the amount of water in your pool. Another good reason for this is that you will need this number if you treat the water for chloramines or add mosquito dunks—so you can deliver the proper dosage. To plan accurately, you need to know two things:

WHAT IS THE SURFACE AREA OF YOUR POND? Surface area can be figured out more-or-less accurately by multiplying Length × Width. (Don't go by the size of the preformed liner or empty pond, because the finished pond will be somewhat smaller, due to the edging materials.) You don't need to obsess over perfectly accurate calculations, but you certainly should have a ballpark figure.

WHAT IS THE CAPACITY OF YOUR POND? This refers to how much water it will hold when filled. The volume of water required to fill even a moderate-size pool may surprise you, but this is mainly a one-time job (or, a once-each-spring job, if you empty or lower the pool water in fall). If you install a pre-formed liner, the supplier can give you the number; for a flexible liner or cement pool, you'll have to do some math. The exact figure may be tricky to come up with; curves (especially if there are several), sloping sides, and shelves for marginals can throw off your number. For irregular dimensions, use the closest average dimen-

CAN'T MISS TIP:

DON'T PANIC!

A newly installed pool will always experience a flush of algae at first, until your plants begin to fill out, "good bacteria" gets established, and algal growth subsides naturally. Whatever you do, do not succumb to impatience or panic and empty the pool and start over! The repeated introduction of fresh water only sets the process back to the beginning. For more information on coping with algae, see Chapter 3.

sion. Also, bear in mind that objects placed in the pool, from potted plants to a pump, will cause some water displacement.

Here are the formulas. One cubic foot of water = 7.5 gallons of water. (For metric conversions, 1 cubic foot of water = 28.3 cubic centimeters.) To get the volume of water for a square or rectangular pool, multiply Length × Width × Depth × 7.5. For a circular pool, multiply Radius × Radius × Depth × 7.5. (If you are dealing with an irregularly-shaped pool, simplify your math by figuring out average dimensions before applying this formula.)

CAN'T MISS TIP:

QUICK TRICK

Visit your water meter before you start filling your pool and note the reading; then check it again when you're done. This will give you a very good idea of how much water the pool requires.

The Right Number of Plants

As you formulate a plan for which plants you will be growing, and how many of each, it is important to adhere to the two-thirds coverage rule, and it is nice to have some variety. Knowing your pond's surface area (discussed above) is key.

What is the probable mature size of each plant? This information is available from the place where you buy the plant—if it's not on a tag, be sure to ask. Mature dimensions are also listed with the recommended-plant list in Chapter 4 and also in specialty catalog descriptions. Realize that results may vary in your own garden, depending on the size of the pot you grow a plant in, the amount of sun and fertilizer (if any) each one gets, and the length of your growing season.

The idea here is to discover, and accommodate, the space needs of each plant. In this way, you can choose an appropriate number of plants and feel confident that each one will thrive and that the planted pool, once up and running, will prosper and look terrific.

The Ecological Role of Submerged Plants

These vital underwater plants may not be obvious to the casual admirer of your water garden, but they are the unsung heroes. Don't overlook them! They help keep the pool water clear by filtering out nutrients that algae would otherwise feed upon.

They also produce oxygen during the daytime hours (which is why some suppliers and reference books persist in calling them, semi-accurately, "oxygenators"). Their presence is a boon to your fish population because they contribute oxygen to the pool

Submerged plants add oxygen to your water garden and help keep algae at bay.

environment and their trailing foliage and roots provide a place for fish to hide from predators as well as an ideal place to spawn.

Most submerged plants are grassy-looking plants that aren't especially attractive, but then again, they aren't readily visible either, so it's not a worry. They're available from any water-garden or aquarium supplier; a few good ones are profiled in Chapter 4.

How many? A tried-and-true formula is one or two bunches (several plants each) of submerged plants for every 2 square feet of surface area. But experiment to find out what works best for your water garden. Generally speaking, it's better to have too many than too few.

Creatures of the Water Garden

One big reason many of us want a pond in our backyard is so that we can enjoy aquatic creatures, especially fish. Their presence makes the scene seem more alive and more enchanting—koi will actually come and eat from your hand! It's also worth adding a few creatures that contribute to your pool's good health, such as scavenging snails.

And then there are the uninvited guests—"if you build it, they will come," as the saying goes! Frogs may be welcome (and their tadpoles), as will flitting dragonflies and perhaps a sunning turtle, but hungry birds and clumsy raccoons will not be. (For advice on preventing and dealing with water-garden pests, please see Chapter 3.)

The Role of Fish

Darting fish are always a fun and attractive sight, adding to the pleasure of having a water garden. Their presence is practical as well—they're an important ingredient in a pool's ecological balance. Like the scavengers that they are, they nibble algae and organic debris, including decaying plant stems and foliage. They also eat pest insects, particularly mosquito larvae—and nobody wants their backyard pond to become a breeding ground, especially if West Nile or the EEE virus (Eastern Equine Encephalitis) is a problem in your area. Last but not least, the carbon dioxide that is a by-product of their respiration is immediately available to your plants.

Here is where knowing your pond's capacity comes into play. For common goldfish, the formula is 1 inch of fish per 5 gallons (20 liters) of water. Koi, because they are so much larger, should be added more sparingly, 1 inch per 10 gallons (40 liters) of water. (Koi longer than 6 inches need substantially more water.) Over time, of course, your own experience may counsel a few more or less.

Wait to add fish until you are sure your pond is chlorine- or chloramines-free (see page 31), perhaps a week after the plants have gone in.

HOW TO ADD FISH: Assuming you purchased disease-free fish from a reputable supplier, they can go in when the water is ready. (Any concerns? Quarantine them for several weeks in a bowl or aquarium to observe them and make sure they are healthy.) Never toss fish into the pool—at the very least, the temperature change may be a shock. Instead, float them on the surface in a water-filled baggie for an hour or so, out of direct sunlight, and then release them into their new home.

In Defense of Cheap Fish

If you're a beginner, you'd be wise to start off with inexpensive fish (such as goldfish, comets, or shubunkins) and see how that goes before investing in more expensive ones. There are three good reasons for this.

1. You can discover if there are herons or other hungry predatory birds in your neighborhood, and, if so, learn ways to combat them (see Chapter 3 for some ideas).
2. You'll learn how much food and how much waste a certain number of fish generate and can adjust the population accordingly.
3. Pricier, more exotic fish tend to be less tough, that is, not as cold-hardy and perhaps in need of more highly filtered water than the cheap ones.

A Few Words About Koi

These large, brightly-colored carp relatives are very popular, and no wonder—they're beautiful and fascinating. They can even be trained to come to the edges of

CAN'T MISS TIP:

ONE FISH, TWO FISH

Don't forget that your fish will grow and place an increasing burden on the pool environment and filtering system. You can also expect them to multiply. So it's a good idea to occasionally net extras and find new homes for them.

Koi will come to greet you if you feed them regularly.

CAN'T MISS TIP:

THE BEST ARE BRIGHTEST!

Whether ordinary goldfish or fancy koi, seek out fish with colorful markings. These show up best in dark water. Patterned ones, and even all-white ones, are easiest to see.

your pond and eat fish snacks right out of your hand! So tame and intelligent are these fish (compared to other fish, anyway) that some people give them names and consider them pets. But before you take the plunge, there are some things you should know:

■ They grow big, and thus require a big, deep pool! Some can even reach 3 feet in length. Depending on the size of your water garden, you may only be able to support a few. Recommended water depth is 3 to 5 feet.

■ They eat a lot. Special koi pellets are available where the fish are sold, and you can supplement their diet with treats like lettuce and cabbage or even small pieces of watermelon. Smaller and younger koi eat at least once a day, while large ones need breakfast, lunch, and dinner! Do keep your koi well fed, or they may nibble on your water plants!

■ They generate a lot of waste, yet they are happier in clean water. So it's wise to install a special filter for them, for their health as well as the clarity of your water. (See Chapter 1, page 42, for information on the various sorts of water filters.)

■ They are long-lived. Assuming you take good care of them and are able to keep predators away, they might even outlive you! Some varieties have been known to live up to fifty years.

Snails help achieve balance in your water garden's ecology.

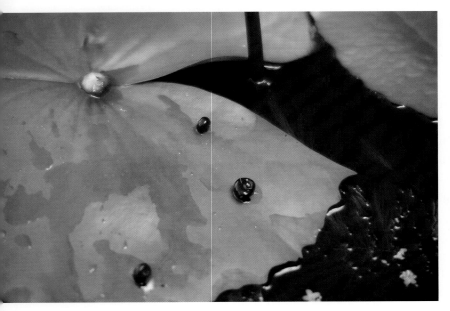

Other Desirable Pond Creatures

Other water-loving creatures, whether introduced by you or appearing on their own, can make important and useful contributions to your pond's ecology. Scavengers like snails are little unsung heroes—they are rarely seen but perform valuable functions in the life of your water garden. Not only do they eat algae, but they also consume decaying plant tissue and other pool debris . . . they are the little "vacuum cleaners" of the pond.

The most common choice is fresh-water snails, available from water-garden suppliers and pet stores that supply aquarium hobbyists. You may also wish to try freshwater clams or freshwater mussels. Make sure you are buying ones that don't eat plants!

If frogs appear in your water garden long enough to lay eggs, you'll welcome the help of tadpoles . . . in moderate numbers. These little creatures tend to eat a lot of insects.

The general formula for such scavengers is one or two per square foot (per 30 square centimeters) of surface area. Wait to add these until you are sure your pond is free of chlorine or chloramines (see page 31).

Pot water-garden plants in heavy soil, never in store-bought potting mix.

Planting Techniques and Tips

Before stocking, make sure you know the surface area and capacity of your pond (see the formulas above) so you won't overstock. You can always add plants or creatures, refining the mix as you get to know your water garden's needs and personality.

Late spring, as with the rest of your garden, is a popular time to fill your pond or water feature. Don't jump the gun, as too-cold water inhibits plant growth and causes fish and other creatures to be sluggish.

To determine water temperature, obtain a (waterproof) pool thermometer. Just as with a swimming-pool one, you can either dip it in the water to

Many kinds of containers can be used in your water garden.

get a reading, or tie a string to it and let it remain submerged. When the water is 50-60 degrees, add submerged plants, hardy marginals, and hardy waterlilies. When it's 70 to 80 degrees, and stabilized, add tropical marginals, tropical waterlilies, and lotus.

The Case Against Planting in the Pool Bottom

Although growing directly in soil at a pond's bottom is nature's way, it doesn't work well in a home water garden. A substantial layer of soil, muck, or both, at the bottom of your pool leads to dirty water, water that is impossible to keep clear; the problem is even worse if you have fish because they love to stir up the bottom.

In such a setting, the plants themselves can become a maintenance hassle. You'll find it difficult to provide them with optimum planting depths. Those that do get established will do so with a vengeance, spreading wherever they find a foothold and tangling with their fellows until pruning back their invasive growth becomes too difficult. Finally, from an aesthetic point of view, if you plant in the pool's bottom, it's just too hard to control your display and position the plants artfully in relation to one another.

Planting in Pots

The best way to contain plant growth and allow yourself design flexibility at the same time is to grow your water-garden plants in pots (with the exception of floaters and some, not all submerged plants). In nature, waterlilies grow in soil at the bottom of a pond, but the garden hybrids have no trouble adjusting to life in containers.

BIGGER IS BETTER: The key to success is bigger pots, rather than smaller—if a pot is too small, a plant may prosper at first, but will later become cramped and crowded. Here are typical sizes and recommendations:

- 1 gallon ($8 \times 5^5/_8$ inches): dwarf waterlilies, marginal/bog plants
- 2 gallon (10×6 inches): medium-size waterlilies, marginal/bog plants
- $2^1/_2$ gallon shallow (12×6 inches): small lotus, medium to large waterlilies, marginal/bog plants
- $4^1/_2$ gallon (16×7 inches): small lotus, medium to large waterlilies, marginal/bog plants
- 5 gallon (12×9 inches): medium to large waterlilies, marginal/bog plants

- 5 gallon/shallow (22 × 12 × 7 inches): small lotus
- 7 gallon (16 × 11 inches): medium to large waterlilies, marginal/bog plants
- 15 gallon (23 × 10 inches): large waterlilies, large lotus, large or multiple marginal/bog plants

WIDE YET SHALLOW: In the case of waterlilies, because their root systems tend to expand horizontally rather than downward, broad yet shallow pots are ideal. It's fine for marginals as well. This configuration is more stable than tall-and-narrow; the pot can rest easily on a pond bottom, pondside shelf, or raised (but unseen) support.

CLUSTERING MARGINALS: Potted marginal plants (such as irises, umbrella palms, or arrowhead) may be grown in narrower pots if you wish. But the pots should be deep enough to accommodate their root systems and are best grouped or clustered for stability. That is, a pair or trio of containers might help hold one another erect, especially if there's a stiff breeze.

MORE THAN ONE PLANT IN A POT? If you are ambitious, and strong, you can use a big pot and grow two plants side by side in it. For two waterlilies, this would be nearly tub-size in order to be wide enough. And maneuvering something this heavy (one filled with soil and plants) could be hard on

Marginals should be clustered on shelves or supports inside the edge of a water garden.

DELIBERATELY UNDERPOTTING

Underpotting refers to planting a waterlily or other plant in a pot that's a bit too small for it. The theory is that this forces the plant to grow a bit less lustily, producing less expansive foliage but still blooming. Some plants don't mind this, while others sulk. You can experiment to see what works for you, or get the advice of your waterlily vendor. (Also, if a waterlily still prospers when underpotted, this quality is so noted in the plant entries in Chapter 4, but that is by no means a complete list of all such available waterlilies.)

your back. Still, this has the nice advantage of allowing you to closely juxtapose two plants that you feel will look great together. Putting multiple plants in one big pot also works for miniature bog gardens.

DRAINAGE HOLES: Unlike potted plants on dry land, aquatic plant pots lack holes in the bottom. This keeps soil out of your water, and prevents the roots from questing out and running wild. It also keeps fertilizer contained at the root zone. If you choose a pot (such as a large terra-cotta azalea pot) that has a drainage hole, be sure to block it.

PREFERRED POT MATERIALS: A water-garden center or catalog will offer you black mesh or solid plastic pots in various sizes. Plastic or terra-cotta "azalea pots" are also popular with water gardeners because they are wider than deep, but choose big ones. Even plastic laundry tubs can be used for some plants.

The Right Soil for the Job

Unlike other container-grown plants, water garden plants should never be potted in peat-based potting mix such as you use for other potted plants. It lacks the heavy dose of organic matter that aquatic plants love. Also, it is too lightweight to hold its own

SIGNS THAT YOU'VE UNDERPOTTED

If, after a few weeks on display, a potted waterlily or other plant isn't flowering well or at all, or if its growth seems stunted, you may have underpotted it in too small a container.

Or perhaps a plant is growing pretty well but keeps toppling over due to the weight and heft of its topgrowth—this is also a sure sign you've underpotted it.

Just to confirm your suspicions, you can haul it out of the water and check to see if roots are bursting out. They may be coming over the side.

When this happens, there are two remedies:

1. Divide the plant and return one healthy portion to the original pot (and pot up other pieces to place elsewhere in your display or to give away).
2. Repot it in a substantially larger container.

ELEVATING WATER PLANTS

Although the typical water garden is 18 to 24 inches deep, this is more than enough for most aquatic plants. You do want them immersed, but not too deep! A foot under the water's surface is fine for most waterlilies, tropical or hardy. The needs of marginals vary, from 2 inches to much deeper, depending on the plant's habit. It's the roots that need to be underwater; avoid submerging foliage.

When you need to elevate a plant, here are some ideas. Just remember that whatever you provide for support, it should be stable and not wobbly, and you should never use materials that can puncture or damage your liner or leach into the water, adversely affecting water clarity, quality, or even pH.

- Side shelves accommodate potted marginals well, provided they're wide enough to hold the pots.
- Bricks...the advantage here is that you can make a pile of exactly the right dimensions and height for the pot.
- Cinder or concrete block, well-rinsed so as not to make the water too alkaline.
- An empty, overturned pot, particularly if it is the same size or larger than the one it's supporting.
- Milk or file crates (black ones are best because they are much less visible).

Here's what it looks like before it goes into the water.

underwater, leaching into the water and contributing to floating scum.

Instead, you must use a medium that is closer to what nature provides in pond muck—rich, heavy topsoil or garden loam. There may be no need to buy it; you can harvest it right from a corner of your flower or vegetable garden. (If you do buy it, be sure to get "topsoil," not "potting soil.")

The Wonderful World of Water Plants

If you've always been, shall we say, a "terrestrial gardener," you are in for a treat. Or rather, many treats. The plants

CAN'T MISS TIP:

USE BALLAST

Even with heavy garden soil, a potted plant may need extra weight to stay submerged and in its assigned place. An easy way to assure extra stability is to put a few rocks in the bottom of the pot first—they will act as ballast.

that enjoy life in water come in all sorts of colors (flower as well as foliage), sizes, shapes, heights, and textures. With careful and creative choosing, you can make a fantastic display.

We'll start with the bigger, deeper-water, middle-of-the-pool plants first, on the assumption that you'll want at least one of these and can build the rest of the show around them: waterlilies and lotus. These come in both smaller and larger sizes, so even a small pool or container ought to be able to host at least one; bigger pools can accommodate several.

The next biggest water plants are the marginals, or bog plants, the ones that do best at the edges of your display in shallower water. There's a broad range of choices—some are valued for their flowers (or seedheads), others for their foliage, some for both.

Whatever space you have left over on the surface can be devoted to various smaller-sized floating plants, which enjoy deep or shallow water. And finally, you'll want to include some submerged plants, which contribute some oxygen to the water by day and perhaps shelter for fish and snails, if you have them.

For all of these, there's shopping advice and planting and placement instructions in the next few pages—all you need to know to go from falling in love with a plant to installing it in your water display.

Please note: For specific details about specific plants that interest you, please turn to Chapter 4's Plant Directory, or study the offerings at a water-garden nursery or catalog.

A small container can easily support one small blooming waterlily plant.

Star of the Show: Waterlilies

The truth is, these exquisite beauties are practically synonymous with water gardening—which is why so much space is devoted to them here as well as in water-garden catalogs and nurseries. You don't have to include them—it's certainly possible to have an attractive and colorful display without them—but they are so lovely and so satisfying to grow, why miss out?

Provided the spot you've chosen gets six or so hours of sun a day, you can enjoy waterlilies in every color of the rainbow. They are both easy and rewarding to grow, blooming gloriously all summer long once they are established. Begin your shopping by learning about your candidate's needs and habits. (Consult the descriptions in Chapter 4 as well as the listings in catalogs and reference books.)

There are two kinds of waterlilies, hardy and tropical. Not surprisingly, gardeners in colder climates have more success with hardies, and gardeners with long, hot summers report spectacular results with tropicals. Even so, either or both can be grown well in most parts of North America. Mixing and matching them works well. Growing only one sort is also fine.

There is a wide variety of waterlilies, but of primary concern to you at the outset should be plant size. Some waterlilies are naturally small, spreading out

But a container display without a waterlily will also look beautiful.

TWO KINDS OF WATERLILIES

At first glance, the differences may not be dramatic, but once you know more, the contrast is obvious. Below are the general characteristics (but bear in mind, as with so many other plants, there are occasional exceptions to the rule).

Hardy
- flowers (usually) float on the water surface
- single flowers as well as many per plant
- smaller-sized flowers
- usually unscented
- grow from a horizontal rhizome
- no night-bloomers
- lilypads are plain green or slightly mottled
- in winter they slow down and go dormant, but can tolerate freezing conditions
- there are no viviparous ones
- flower colors are white, yellow, red, pink, salmon

Tropical
- flowers rise above the water surface
- many flowers per plant
- larger-sized flowers
- usually scented
- grow from a roundish tuber
- some are night-bloomers (open in late afternoon or evening and remain open partway into the following morning)
- lilypads may be lightly or heavily mottled, or bronze/maroon
- in winter cannot tolerate cold (in cold climates, treat as an annual or overwinter indoors)
- some varieties are viviparous
- flower-color range also includes shades of purple and blue

left: **T**ropical waterlily blooms are raised above the surface of the water.

right: **H**ardy waterlily blooms float on the water surface.

their pads to cover an area only 4 to 6 feet wide, while others, given a chance, will become enormous, spreading up to 20 feet across. Stock your pool according to mature plant estimates, no matter how small the plants seem on arrival. If you must have one that is too big, you can try underpotting it.

The Role of Waterlilies

Waterlilies perform several important functions in the world of your water garden. The pads provide shade that inhibits algae growth. Their presence keeps the water temperature cooler and stable, while preventing excessive evaporation. They also shelter fish from predators. And last but not least, waterlilies contribute to your water garden's overall health by producing oxygen via photosynthesis. Few water gardens should be without them.

VIVIPAROUS WATERLILIES

This term is used to describe waterlilies—some tropical ones, to be exact—that produce new little "piggyback" plantlets in the center of their leaves, at the node where the leaf meets its stalk. For most home water gardeners, this characteristic is merely a curiosity, though it's simple to harvest the plantlets and grow them into new plants. To do this, gently tear or cut away the little plant from the big leaf and lay it (it may have tiny roots or will soon develop them) on the surface of a flat of moist builder's sand and peat. Keep it submerged, and be sure

Here is a viviparous waterlily pad.

the flat is warm and out of direct sunlight. Slowly but surely a new waterlily plant will grow. Later, when the tiny plant is established, you can pot it up and place it in your pool. The length of time this process takes varies greatly, depending on the variety and the growing conditions. The youngster will look exactly like the adult.

SHADE-TOLERANT WATERLILIES

The majority of waterlilies need plentiful sunshine to do well (six or so hours per day), but some can get by with as little as three hours.

Generally speaking, blue-hued waterlilies do better than most in spots where there is some shade. The larger-flowered tropical 'Director George T. Moore' tolerates some shade, as does the smaller tropical 'Dauben'. Some yellow ones to consider include: hardy 'Joey Tomocik', hardy 'Chromatella', and hardy 'Charlene Strawn'. Red-hued ones actually may hold their color a little longer with less exposure to hot sun (generally speaking, they don't do well in hot climates). Examples are hardy 'Attraction', hardy 'Escarboucle', and hardy 'Lucida'.

Shopping for a Waterlily

Mail-order suppliers ship waterlily rootstocks bare root, that is, not potted, usually with a few leaves intact. Garden centers carry them potted. Either way, you may see some tiny lime-green or bronze leaves emerging from the plant's growing point, or crown.

It is important that the plant never dry out! So keep it in a plastic bag till you get it home (with a bit of water or a damp rag or paper towel). And if you can't plant it immediately, tuck that bag into the refrigerator or other cool place.

Whether you buy a waterlily locally or via mail order, you should check it over carefully prior to planting, just to make sure that it is in good health and ready to thrive in your water display.

Waterlily roots should be white and crisp. If they are black, soggy, matted, or smell bad, they are probably rotten and not viable and must be

This a tropical waterlily tuber and root system.

A hardy waterlily grows from a rhizome.

removed with a sharp, clean knife. If there are only a few roots in this condition, it shouldn't be a problem.

Be sure to check for hitchhikers such as snails and weeds. Snails may be welcome, as they are good pond scavengers. Duckweed is nearly impossible to remove from a pond and you don't really have to—it's a nice addition to a water garden, at least in moderation.

How to Plant a Waterlily

Tropical waterlilies grow from small roundish tubers, while the hardies grow from long, thick rhizomes. Plant both types in wide, shallow pots of heavy garden soil. Aside from placement of the rootstock, the planting process is identical.

Hardy waterlilies can be placed in water as cool as 50 degrees F without trauma. Tropicals, as you might expect, really prefer warmer water temperatures. If you put a tropical waterlily into water that is too cool, you may shock it, delaying or preventing growth and blooming. Wait until the water in your pool has warmed to at least 70 degrees F.

Potting is a muddy job! So do it someplace where you can hose off the area when you are finished, such as a patio. (Having the hose close by is very helpful.) And wear gloves to protect your hands and arms, if you wish.

1. PREPARE' THE POT. Fill the container one-third full with soil. (You can put gravel on the bottom of the pot to help weight it.) Pause and insert a waterlily fertilizing tablet (available from water-garden suppliers; for more on these and some alternatives, consult Chapter 3). Some water gardeners crush the tablet and mix it evenly through the soil, but this is not essential. Then, to eliminate any air pockets, drench the soil.

2. POT THE ROOTSTOCK. For a hardy waterlily: Set the rhizome, roots down, in the pot at a 45-degree angle. Position it so the plant has room to elongate across the pot and so that the crown points up. For maximum growing room, place the opposite end (the end without the growing point) flush against the side of the pot. For a tropical waterlily: Set the tuber in the center of the pot, roots down.

CAN'T MISS TIP:

MOVING SLOWLY

Many waterlilies ultimately prefer to be about a foot below the water's surface, so gradually move it into deeper water after it's established and the water warms up. Within a few weeks, it should have adjusted to its new home. New leaves will soon begin to appear, and shortly thereafter the first blossoms should make their debut.

3. **TOP OFF.** Now add more soil to the pot, but do so gently, taking care not to harm the plant and to leave the growing point free of soil. Fill to within an inch or two of the rim. To avoid air pockets, firm the soil with your fist as you go. Water the pot once more, taking care not to dislodge your work. Then spread a layer of small stones or pea gravel over the soil surface (again, staying clear of the growing point), an inch or two thick. This prevents soil from washing away in the pool and keeps fish from dislodging the dirt. Tip: If you have koi, add rocks over the gravel for extra insurance.

4. **SLOWLY LOWER THE POT INTO PLACE.** Lower the pot gradually and at an angle to allow any air bubbles to escape and to keep the gravel layer from sliding off. Then gently set it on its base or support. To get the new plant off to a good start, place it 6 to 8 inches below the water surface at first. This allows it to start growing in warmer water. As the plant grows, you can lower it a few inches at a time deeper into the pool. Finally, if the plant has a few leaves, carefully position them so they float on the surface of the water.

Planting for your water garden is much like planting for any other part of your garden.

Be sure you place a potted waterlily at the correct water depth with stones or pebbles on the surface so the soil doesn't drift away.

Before setting your heart on the exotic lotus, be sure it will grow in your area.

The Lowdown on Lotus

Before you get your heart set on growing the exotic-looking lotus, be sure you can meet its needs. Although the plant can be grown almost anywhere in North America, for it to produce those spectacular flowers and pods, it needs warm temperatures. A short summer won't do—lotuses really need two or even three consecutive months of temperatures over 80 degrees F.

Also, don't expect it to bloom for you its first year, though it may, especially if you are heavy-handed with fertilizer—lotuses are greedy feeders. The second year will be better. (But please note that lotuses never bloom as prolifically as waterlilies.)

Size is an important issue as well. Some varieties of lotus, when mature, can spread 10 to 12 feet or more, and its tall-stalked leaves can shoot up to 7 feet! So you either need a large pool or a big container, or try a dwarf lotus, which can be half the size. For recommended lotus varieties, browse Chapter 4.

One nice plus about lotuses is the fact that they tolerate shade pretty well, as long as they get enough warmth. So they are certainly an option if you plan a water feature in a spot that doesn't get full sun all day.

LOTUS FOR THE LEAVES

Though it's easy to become enamored of the glorious flowers, lotus leaves are a show in their own right. They're green with a hint of blue (like some hostas) and have a unique texture. If water splashes on them, droplets bead up and roll around like quicksilver. So it's certainly possible to enjoy a lotus whether it's blooming or not.

Lotus Rootstocks: Handle with Care!

A lotus tuber looks a bit like a double banana, with one or two buds. The entire structure is extremely fragile and brittle. So it must be handled with great care. If the growing end is accidentally broken off, you might as well throw the whole thing away, sadly, as the remaining section will rot.

When you obtain a good, healthy-looking lotus rootstock—in the spring since they aren't sold at other times—don't delay. Plant it as early in the growing season as you can, before it starts sending out all sorts of runners and becomes even more tricky to handle.

How to Plant a Lotus

1. PREPARE THE CONTAINER. For a lotus, the larger the container, the better. For regular lotuses, this means a big tub (24 × 9 inches is fine); the dwarf kinds can be grown in something smaller, such as 16 × 7 inches. Fill it to within a few inches of the rim, with heavy garden soil. A high clay content is fine. (No manure, though—it can burn the fragile, fussy tuber.)

2. POT THE TUBER. Once you've filled the pot with soil, use your finger to trace a little trough in the top of the soil. Gingerly lay the tuber horizontally into this trough, taking care to leave the growing end exposed. Cover the rest, the thickest part, with an inch of additional soil.

3. TOP OFF. Finish the job by carefully sprinkling a layer of pea gravel or rocks over the surface—leaving only the growing tip exposed. Don't use material that has limestone in it, though, because lotuses are sensitive to its alkaline residue. If you're worried about the tuber floating away, carefully place a heavier, flat stone over the main part to anchor it down.

4. LOWER THE POT INTO THE WATER. Lotuses like shallower water than do waterlilies, so a support that keeps the pot at the right height is going to be necessary. Start it off submerged only an inch or two, gradually lowering over the ensuing week to a depth of about 4 inches. While lotuses can be grown a foot below the water's surface, less is generally better.

There are myriad good choices, some with dramatic foliage (like taro and variegated canna), some with tall, thin profiles (like papyrus), and many with pretty flowers (especially the moisture-loving irises).

5. WAIT TO FERTILIZE. The first floating leaves should make an appearance about a month after the water has reached a nice, stable 80 degrees F. They will be followed by the normal aerial leaves. At this point, you may poke holes here and there and insert the same fertilizer tablets that you use for waterlilies (see Chapter 3 for more on fertilizer options). Lotuses are heavy feeders, so it's fine to use four to six tablets at a time.

Flowers may or may not appear the first season, as mentioned earlier. If you want the intriguing seedpods that follow, don't cut off the flower—wait for it to dry out. They're a popular decorative element in dried-flower arrangements, as is or painted.

More on Marginals

A marginal—sometimes called a "bog" plant—is a plant that, in nature, grows on the sides of a pond or in a damp area, hence the name. Such plants are also good candidates for shallow water in a home water garden. They can supply "vertical interest" as well as variety and color. As in the wild, they look best on the perimeters of the water and thus help integrate your pool into the landscape around it. (Not surprisingly, a number of them can also thrive on the banks of your pool; see "Pondside Landscaping" below.)

There are myriad good choices, some with dramatic foliage (like taro and variegated canna), some with tall, thin profiles (like papyrus), and many with pretty flowers (especially the moisture-loving irises). You can use just one kind or distribute various ones throughout your display. For more ideas and information, browse the listings in Chapter 4, as well as the offerings at water-garden nurseries and catalogs. Or try the "moist soil" section at any well-stocked garden center.

Because their basic need for water has been met since they are part of a water garden, these plants require little work to maintain. It's best to grow them in pots, not only to contain any possibility of rampant growth, but also to give you the flexibility to move them about or even remove them if you wish. Even fertilizing is not especially necessary. Marginal plants make great, low-maintenance assets, and no water garden should be without them!

Note that marginals of tropical origin should not be placed in water colder than 70 degrees F. All marginals, tropical or hardy, should prosper and even flower their first year in your water garden.

How to Plant a Marginal

1. SELECT THE RIGHT POT. The sizes of marginal plants vary, but they all need ample room for their root systems. Choose a substantial and stable container, especially if the plant gets top-heavy over time. Two-gallon nursery pots will work (see also the list of pot sizes on page 66 above).

2. PREPARE THE CONTAINER. Fill it, as you do for other water-garden plants, with heavy, organically rich garden soil (never standard potting mix, which is too light and floats away!). Tuck in some balanced fertilizer, if you wish, particularly to encourage bountiful blooms.

3. POT UP THE PLANT. Pop it out of the container it came in, hose off the dirt, and gently untangle dense roots and spread them apart. (If some break off, don't worry; so long as plenty remain, the plant will be fine.) Remove any black, broken, or rotten-looking roots, of course. Press the soil down with your thumbs all around to prevent air pockets and anchor the plant well in place; do not crowd or smother the plant's crown, however. Fill to within an inch or two of the rim. Water well.

4. ADD A GRAVEL LAYER. Pour in a few handfuls of small pebbles or rocks, again avoiding the plant's crown. This will hold the soil in place and protect the plant from nuzzling fish.

5. PLACE IN THE POND. Lower the potted plant carefully into the water to allow air bubbles to escape, onto a support or side shelf. Most require no more than an inch or two of water over the top of the gravel layer.

Placement of Marginal Plants

Marginals are not deep-water plants. Most are perfectly happy with "wet feet" but "dry ankles," meaning that they really only need an inch or two of water over their crown. So support to lift them off the bottom is almost always necessary, at least at the outset, whether you are planting them in a small pool or adding them to a mixed container.

Because of their vertical growth habit, these plants really look best at the sides of your pool, where they make

CAN'T MISS TIP:

ON THE ROCKS

Many marginals can be planted in nothing but gravel or large pebbles (that is, no soil). This not only weights them down, it slows their growth and compels them to take all their nutrients from the water. This technique is particularly worthwhile in larger pools or ones with lots of plants—and it means less maintenance for you.

a visual transition possible from the life of the pond to the surrounding garden. They are harder to care for out in the middle of the water, too—harder to reach for grooming or fertilizing, more trouble to put back upright if they fall over.

Also because of the vertical growth habit of many marginals, they are more apt to topple in a breeze or during a summer storm than their lower-growing, floating-leaf companions. Pond visitors, including pest ones like raccoons, may also knock them over. For this reason, you should make a habit of checking on them often, righting them as soon as possible after the disturbance, and replacing the gravel layer on their soil surface, if need be.

You can prevent toppling problems in four ways:

1. Add ballast to the bottom of the pot, before adding dirt and the plant.
2. Set the container of each marginal on a support that is broader than the pot it's in. This gives more stability. Common supports include bricks, flat-topped rocks, cement blocks, file crates, and overturned, larger pots. (Clay, of course, being heavier, is better than plastic.)
3. Group marginals on supports that will also be grouped, or use one large, broad support that holds several potted marginals. There is safety in numbers, it seems—clustering allows marginals to support one another so they are less likely to all fall over.
4. Place several pots in a laundry or similar-sized tub, filling the tub if not tightly then at least as full as you can. Then set this tub on a shelf or support, out of sight but still effective.

Information on Floaters

These are a group of free-floating plants that can add a lot to a pool, for very little effort. Individual plants can be quite tiny, as with duckweed, or rather large, as with water hyacinth. Some, such as water clover, owe their appeal to their intriguing foliage (that is, they either don't or rarely flower, or their flowers are too small or fleeting to be of interest). Others add charming little flowers to their floating show, such as frogbit's profusion of tiny white blossoms.

This picture of water lettuce and duckweed shows that floaters come in different sizes.

What this diverse group has in common is an ability to grow without soil. Their roots dangle down from beneath their leaves into the water below and manage to derive what nutrients they need. And they have helpful qualities to offer your water garden. Their leaves help shade the water, which inhibits algae growth (by limiting sunlight on the water's surface and having a cooling effect on the water) and creates shelter for fish.

All floaters prosper in full sun. But some tolerate part-day shade and still manage to bloom, including bogbean, *Menyanthes trifoliata*, and water hyacinth, *Eichhornia crassipes*, (where they are not banned, that is; see their listing in Chapter 4 for details). This may interest you if you want color in a partially shaded water-garden display and waterlilies aren't an option. Most floaters also tend to prefer still water, so they aren't a good choice if you have moving water (a stream or waterfall) or a fountain. In such settings, they tend to clump up or get pushed off to the edges.

For more details on various floaters and their characteristics, see Chapter 4, and also browse the offerings at water-garden nurseries.

How to Install Floaters

Planting couldn't be simpler. After you purchase them and get them home, trim off dead or damaged parts and rehydrate the plants for a few hours in a bucket of lukewarm water. Then, just toss them into the water.

Don't install too many. They'll reproduce and increase their numbers with no effort or intervention from you. Ideally, you shouldn't let them have more than a half to two-thirds coverage in a pool. More than that, and they start to choke out sunlight and other plants.

How to Manage Floaters

While it's nice to have a plant in your water garden that requires virtually no effort on your part to thrive and look good, beware. Many floaters really thrive and before you know it, are overpopulated. Keep after them. Surplus is easily scooped out, either by hand or with a net.

Never, ever toss unwanted floaters into a natural or even man-made waterway! This will give their free-growing, free-multiplying ways far too much freedom. A number of floaters have become pests, choking out native vegetation, upsetting the natural food chain, and even clogging waterways so boats can hardly get through anymore. (As a result, in some states, some

WARNING: INVASIVE PLANTS!

Some popular water-garden plants—primarily floaters and submerged plants, often exotic plants of tropical origin—have proven to be terrible pests when they escape the bounds of the home garden. Although they grow lustily in your pond, you can still manage them. Imagine, however, what happens when they get loose in much bigger areas and reproduce uncontrollably. This is why you must never dispose of your extras anywhere near natural or man-made waterways. But even if you are careful, a visiting bird or even the wind can carry pieces or seeds into such areas, and the problems can start.

Invasive water plants are now illegal and banned in many states. Local nurseries can't sell them, and mail-order nurseries can't ship them to you. You can be cited for possessing them in a home garden. This is particularly true in areas where a mild climate allows them to thrive unchecked. Florida, California, Oregon, North and South Carolina, and Texas, for instance, have extensive lists. (Gardeners in cold climates may still legally be able to grow some of these because freezing weather kills off the plants every winter.)

All this doesn't change the fact that some of these pests are attractive-looking plants. But resist the urge to cheat and get them if they are banned or on your state's "Invasive Plants" list. (To find out for certain, contact your state's Natural Heritage Program or the nearest office of the Nature Conservancy.) There are comparable substitutes that are attractive and don't endanger ecosystems.

"Banned" status varies from state to state, and can change from one year to the next as state and federal biologists monitor their status, but here are the most commonly outlawed water-loving plants:

- **anacharis** (*Egeria densa*)
- **flowering rush** (*Butomus umbellatus*)
- **hydrilla** (*Hydrilla verticillata*)
- **parrot's feather** (*Myriophyllum aquaticum*)
- **purple loosestrife** (*Lythrum salicaria*)
- **water lettuce** (*Pistia stratiotes*)
- **water hawthorn** (*Aponogeton distachyos*)
- **water hyacinth** (*Eichhornia crassipes*)
- **water milfoil** (*Myriophyllum spicatum*)
- **yellow flag** (*Iris pseudacorus*)

are outlawed—see the box, Warning: Invasive Plants! above.) Instead, toss your discards safely onto your compost pile or dig them into your vegetable garden or flowerbeds.

A number of floaters are of tropical origin. This makes them exotics in North America. So their spread can go unchecked by natural predators—yet another reason never to allow them to get into your area's streams, lakes, or reservoirs. This also means that, if you garden in a cold climate, they will die over the winter. If you want to save some for next year, simply reserve a few pieces and keep them in an indoor heated aquarium until next spring.

Submerged Plants

These humble plants can play an important role in your water garden, as they produce oxygen by day (hence they are sometimes referred to as "oxygenators"). The oxygen helps keep your pond healthy, particularly your fish population. They are usually plain green and either grassy (species of *Vallisneria*) or made up of whorls of tiny leaves on long stems (like anacharis, *Egeria densa*, and hornwort, *Cabomba caroliniana*). If they look familiar, maybe you've seen them waving underwater in hobby aquariums.

Every water garden, even a tub display, can benefit from the addition of these plants. You do not really need to be concerned with what they look like because they tend to remain below the water's surface, out of sight but quietly making their contribution.

A few are vigorous growers, however, and may reach the surface and create a presence—a classic example is the popular parrot's feather, *Myriophyllum aquaticum*. So keep an eye out and be prepared to trim back or yank out some stems if your submerged plants start to exceed their bounds.

Submerged plants can add texture to your pond.

How to Plant a Submerged Plant

1. PREPARE THE PLANTS. These plants are usually sold in bunches of several plants each. Separate them into groups of two or three plants, discarding any that have yellowing foliage or otherwise don't look healthy. If their ends look bedraggled, use a sharp, clean knife to make a fresh cut at the base of each stalk. This is best done underwater, just as if you were preparing a bouquet of fresh-cut flowers for a vase.

2. POT UP. Submerged plants perform better and are easier to control when grown in pots. A 1-quart plastic nursery pot is usually sufficient. Fill it with builder's sand. (They may also be grown in the same soil you use when potting up your other water-garden plants, but they don't

need the soil for nutrition since they get that from the water.) All you do is stick the cut end into the growing medium, about 2 inches or so deep is usually sufficient. Don't worry about the lack of roots—they'll develop quickly.

3. TOP OFF. As with other potted water-garden plants, you need to spread a layer (an inch or less thick) of pea gravel over the potting medium's surface to keep the soil from drifting away underwater and to add weight.

4. LOWER INTO THE WATER. Potted submerged plants can go in the bottom of a container or pond. (They do not need to be raised up on supports.) Just lower them into the water carefully, tipped sideways at first, to allow any air bubbles to escape, then set them on the flat bottom.

In the first day or so after planting, check on the plants. Because they are lightweight, sometimes they slip away and are found floating loose. If this happens, retrieve them and stick them back in their pots. Occasionally one or two will escape anyway and establish themselves in the thin layer of muck that may develop at the bottom of your pool—that's fine, just keep an eye on them so they don't grow too rampantly

Be advised that submerged plants tend to be vigorous growers. In a matter of a week or less, particularly if the water is warm, they will take hold in their pots and start sending out new foliage.

Pondside Landscaping

You'll want to disguise your pool's edge for practical reasons, such as to hide and protect the liner. This process is started by adding rocks, bricks, wood, or other "hardscaping" materials. If you install stonework (mortared in place) or overlay with wooden decking, just remember to allow a stable lip to jut out over the water. (For more ideas and information, please see Chapter 1, "Finishing Touches," page 28.) But you may want to add some plants after that border or boundary is in place because it will go a long way towards helping your water garden fit into the rest of your landscape.

Grassy Banks

If grass is your choice, you may try to plant it as close to the pool edge as possible. The best way to accomplish this is with pieces of sod. Cut fairly small pieces, about a foot long, so you can accommodate the pond's natural

Be advised that submerged plants tend to be vigorous growers. In a matter of a week or less, particularly if the water is warm, they will take hold in their pots and start sending out new foliage.

curves. Once it's all growing strong, you won't be able to tell where the established lawn ended and the new grass edging began.

Grass is one way to edge your water garden.

A perimeter devoted to grass works best—and frankly, looks best—with square or rectangular pools. It is tricky to install lawn around a water garden that has irregular, curving edges, plus maintenance becomes tricky as well (it's almost impossible to mow right up to the edge; even a weed-whacker might not be able to accomplish the neat look you want).

The best away around the challenging installation and maintenance issues is to include a buffer of "hardscape" around your water garden's perimeter, and start the grass just beyond that. This narrow barrier can be made of non-plant materials such as bricks or regular stones or even a border of mulch (but not a loose mulch; that becomes its own maintenance headache, as you might imagine). This also protects the pond liner, which can be unintentionally damaged by a mower or string trimmer.

A few final words of caution: Lawn food (high-nitrogen fertilizer), insecticides, and weed-killers used on lawns are detrimental to pond life. Avoid using these altogether, or at least in the vicinity of your water garden. Even with a raised edge intended to prevent runoff into the pool, these harmful chemicals can enter the water and wreak havoc, killing fish and plants.

Also, take care when you mow your lawn or clip grass close to the water garden, as you sometimes must. Don't let bits of grass get into the water, or if they do, scoop them out with a net.

Edging Plants

CONSIDER THE HABITAT: What is the soil like around the edges of your water garden? When you installed it, did you backfill the area with subsoil? If so, some amending may be in order before pondside plants can prosper— perhaps you can dig in several inches of organic matter, just as you would when adding new plants to, say, a flowerbed. Is the area rather dry or naturally damp? How much sun is there? Again, as with putting plants in anywhere else in your yard, you need to make a match.

CONSIDER THE HABIT: Plants that arch, hang, or cascade are natural choices for the poolside because they soften the transition from garden to water display. They also look more natural. Just be careful not to use ones that grow too tall, especially in the front of your pool or from whichever sides

Marginals add to any water garden, whether it's in the sun or gets some shade.

it is most commonly seen, because they'll restrict access as well as obstruct the view of the water and its contents. Taller ones can go on the far side of the pool, of course. And avoid plants that drop a lot of leaves and spent flowers, if they are to hang over the water.

WHAT TO CHOOSE: Low-maintenance plants are probably best for pondside because they'll fill their roles quickly and leave you free to lavish attention on the water garden itself. Avoid plants that are prone to shedding a lot of foliage or flower petals, or you'll be cleaning up after them on the ground as well as in the adjacent water. "Foliage plants" such as ferns and ornamental grasses are just fine for the job.

Moisture-lovers can be used—among them, candelabra primroses, irises, creeping jenny, and water mint—but don't assume they'll enjoy a continual or adequate supply of damp soil there just because they're near water. Supplemental water may be necessary, particularly if your summer becomes hot and dry.

Many of the moisture-loving marginals that are appropriate for shallow water in your pool are also a good choice for the perimeter planting. Design-wise, they make an effective transition from the pond to the land. They also intuitively "look right," like they belong, because, in natural pond areas, they do. Browse the listings in Chapter 4, or check out the offerings in water-garden nurseries and catalogs as well as general garden centers.

WHEN PLANTING: Place edging plants far enough back from the edge so they'll be able to form adequate root systems and prosper. Container-grown plants, whether in attractive pots above ground, or sunk into the ground, are another option to consider.

Integrate your water display into its surroundings by using vertical-habit plants in the water *and* on the banks.

Maintenance and Trouble-shooting

taking care of a water garden during the height of the growing season is not much different from attending to other parts of your garden. You'll fertilize, prune, ward off pests, and occasionally divide and repot. What you won't have to do, of course, is water. And for that reason alone, maintenance will feel less demanding—no rushing to hydrate wilting flowers on a hot day. In fact, water gardens positively adore hot summer days; waterlilies in particular will bloom with abandon.

As for the rest of the year, you'll have regular start-up and end-of-season chores. Tried-and-true techniques for overwintering the plants, the creatures, and the pool itself are covered in this chapter. You can keep your annual maintenance routine simple, or you may choose to get involved in a more elaborate regimen. Whatever you decide, you'll find the tasks are basic, logical, and fairly simple to execute.

Caring for the Plants

Whether you are tending a large in-ground pool or a small containerized water garden, the maintenance is pretty much the same. Let's take a seasonal approach—there will be more or less work for you to do based on what sorts of plants you choose to grow and how many of each you have.

Water gardens are not totally self-sufficient, but a healthy one does function well without a great deal of intervention on the part of the gardener—giving you more time to simply enjoy its beauty!

Please note that because many lovely water-garden plants are exuberant growers, it is much easier to maintain them if you plant them in pots (see Chapter 2).

Caring for a water garden feels less demanding because one of the key needs of your plants is already met—water.

Summertime is peak season for your water garden. If you can, visit it daily, to enjoy it and also to keep an eye on things.

Summer Maintenance

A healthy, ecologically balanced pool has about two-thirds of its surface covered with plant matter, usually a combination of lilypads and other, smaller plants. Keep an eye on things and take out surplus plants as needed. (Discard unwanted plants and plant parts on your compost pile, or in your flowerbeds or vegetable garden—*never* in natural or man-made waterways because some are extremely invasive!)

When you work in your pond, you may be able to accomplish some things by kneeling on the shore. For other jobs, like fertilizing plants out in the middle, you may have to carefully climb into the water in your shorts or fishing waders. Just watch your step—the bottom may be slippery.

Waterlilies are the star attraction of many water gardens, and they are easy to maintain.

Waterlilies

Make it a practice always to remove spent leaves and flowers; an individual leaf tends to last about three weeks, whereas an individual flower is in its prime for around three or four days. If you leave them, they not only look unsightly but will also eventually break down and rot, adding extra organic matter to the water. Cut them off at the bases of their stalks (use a sharp knife, clippers, or scissors, as tugging with your bare hands might pull them out of their pots, roots and all). Here are some other suggestions for waterlily care in the summer.

Fertilize once a month during the growing season for maximum bloom production. Poke the food down into the pot, well past the gravel layer on the soil surface. (For options, see Food for Water-garden Plants, page 92.)

Be on the lookout for insect pests. Wipe off the bottom of the lilypads periodically to dislodge any eggs that may have been laid there. If you spot aphids on leaves, flowers, or buds, spray them off with the hose and let your fish eat them.

Also watch for crown rot problems, especially in colder climates. Signs that this highly contagious condition has afflicted one of your plants are rotting black stems, buds that fail to open, yellowing lilypads, and an odd smell. Immediately remove and treat or discard affected plants—see page 122 below for details about this disease.

Lotus

Make it a practice always to remove spent leaves, cutting them above the waterline. (If you cut a stem below the waterline or at the tuber, bacterial or fungal infections can reach the tuber and kill the plant.) Also, if you leave spent or bedraggled leaves, they not only look unsightly but also eventually break down and rot, adding extra organic matter to the water.

Lotus flowers last up to four days, usually. Remove spent flower petals so they don't foul the water. Although it can mean fewer blossoms in the long run, most lotus fans can't resist letting the plants "go to seed" so they can enjoy the sight of the intriguing, decorative seedpods.

Fertilize often! Lotuses are notoriously greedy feeders, and even though you've potted them in a large container of organically rich soil, it's not enough. Twice a month, during the growing season, is fine for fertilizing. Just be careful where you insert the plant food, so as to avoid harming the fragile rootstock— this is more of an issue when a lotus is young and newly planted. (For more information on plant food, see Food for Water-garden Plants, page 92.)

Raising water-loving plants in a container is easy and rewarding.

Marginals

Trim back spent and rampant growth. Fertilize monthly only if growth seems small or weak or there are few flowers. Poke the fertilizer well down into the pot, past the gravel layer on the soil surface.

Most of these plants like to have water a few inches over their "feet," so be vigilant about your water level and top off when necessary.

Floaters and Submerged Plants

A few of these plants at the beginning of the growing season can soon burgeon into an overpopulation problem. You don't have to be gentle with them—just yank or scoop out unwanted plants and dispose of them properly. When you are removing excess plants, be careful to extract any small fish or water snails you find lodged in their tangles and return these to the water.

Water plants benefit from regular doses of fertilizer during the growing season—you'll get heartier growth and more flowers.

A single dose of any of most tablet fertilizers will supply enough food for a single waterlily in a gallon pot. Use more for big plants in big pots; use more for lotus plants. Use less for smaller plants and marginals, or if fertilizing more often than once a month.

To deliver the food to a plant's roots, where it is needed, simply tuck or poke the food down into the pot, well past the gravel layer on the soil surface. If necessary, use a dibble, dowel, or broom handle. Be sure to cover the hole when you're done.

The numerical formulations described below refer, as they do with all garden fertilizers, to the relative amounts of nitrogen (N), phosphorus (P), and potassium (K). Nitrogen enhances stem and leaf growth; phosphorus contributes to flower and seed production; potassium ensures general vigor and helps resistance to plant diseases. As for minor (trace) elements, these are also important, especially for waterlily flowering.

- **Tablets:** Available from water-garden suppliers, these are specially formulated to feed aquatic plants. Often a 10-14-8 analysis. Follow the dosage recommendations on the label.

- **Time-release fertilizer:** Agriform™, Osmocote™, or Dynamite™, in 13-13-13 or other formulations. This eliminates the need for repeated fertilizing and so is favored by water gardeners who tend large collections of plants. Wrap a few handfuls in cheesecloth, burlap, or a single layer of newspaper and stuff the wad deep into the pot so it will benefit the roots and also not leak out into the pool water.

- **Conventional granular garden fertilizer**: In 5-10-5, 5-10-10, and 10-6-4 formulations, these can certainly do the trick. (Never use lawn food, which is too high in nitrogen and encourages leafy growth at the expense of bloom, plus it may contain herbicides.) Wrap a few handfuls in cheesecloth, burlap, or a single layer of newspaper and stuff the wad deep into the pot so it will benefit the roots and also not leak out into the pool water.

- **Blood meal or bone meal:** These are best added to the original soil when you first pot a plant. If adding them after potting, wrap in cheesecloth, burlap, or a single layer of newspaper and stuff the wad deep into the pot so it will benefit the roots and also not leak out into the pool water.

- **A handful of well-rotted cow manure:** Never use fresh manure, and use packaged manure only if it is well rotted, or you'll end up with murky water. Wrap in cheesecloth, burlap, or a single layer of newspaper.

- **Fruit tree spikes:** A strong, but slow-release 10-15-15 formulation. Break into walnut-size pieces and insert like tablets.

Please note: Too much N or P will inspire algae growth, but will not harm your fish.

Fall Clean-up

Generally speaking, autumn is a time for the water garden to slow down. And you should let it. Especially, cease fertilizing. The dying foliage will continue to feed the rootstocks, while the increasingly cold water and shorter days will encourage the plants to go dormant. At that point, you can intervene, getting rid of spent foliage and preparing the plants for the coming winter.

If this sounds similar to the way your plants growing out in the rest of your garden behave in the fall, it is. Aquatic plants, no less than others, follow a seasonal cycle.

In all but the shallowest pools and the coldest climates, hardy plants may spend the winter outdoors, though they'll need a little attention first. Some tropicals will continue blooming until killed by frost. So you can either let this happen and then discard them (treat them as annuals) or intervene a bit earlier and save them over the winter indoors.

COLD-WINTER ALERT: Keep plants in the pool until there has been a frost (assuming your area experiences very cold winters).

Hardy Waterlilies, Lotuses, and Marginals

For outdoor overwintering, you will need labels, clippers, gravel.

1. Haul individual plants out of the water and work on them pondside (or, if it's too chilly outdoors, in a garage, greenhouse, or other workspace).
2. Make new name labels and poke each one deep into its pot, so you'll remember all the names come next spring.
3. Chop off and discard all the leaves and stems to within 3 to 5 inches of the plant's crown. Spare any tiny leaves or leaflets you spot emerging from the crown, however, as they are the beginning of next spring's growth.

CAN'T MISS TIP:

WHEN LEAVES BEGIN TO FALL

If you have deciduous trees or shrubs in your yard or nearby, their leaves may fall or get blown into your pool at this time of year, leading to quite a daunting mess. Head this off at the pass by placing netting over the water (anchored around the sides) and cleaning it off when it gets fairly full. Water-garden centers and mail-order suppliers sell lightweight mesh netting that is ideal for coping with this problem.

In autumn, you can either overwinter tender plants or remove them now (thus treating them like annuals). Hardy plants can remain in the water year-round in many areas, with a little preparation.

WATERLILIES AS CUT FLOWERS

The best time to cut a waterlily blossom is the first day it begins to open (but if the green or maroon sepals are still clasping the bud tightly, the flower may not open). Cut each one with scissors or a sharp knife, close to the plant's crown, to get the longest possible stem. It will continue to open and unfurl its exceptional beauty indoors in a vase of lukewarm water.

You'll notice that the petals will close up each evening and re-open in the morning. The show should last at least three days, which is the normal lifespan of a waterlily blossom out in the garden, too.

Waterlilies make spectacular bouquet flowers. They will open each morning and close each evening, just as they do outdoors—for a period of about three days.

4. If necessary, replenish the gravel topping on the soil surface.
5. Return the pots to the pool, placing them on the bottom of the deepest part, where they are least likely to freeze or suffer from temperature fluctuations.

For indoor overwintering, you will need scissors or clippers, labels, weed-free straw or clean glass jars/plastic baggies and damp peat moss.

If your pool freezes to the bottom, or you fear it might, play it safe. After their "haircut," top off individual plants with a handful of straw and store them in a dark, cool—but not freezing—place such as the garage or basement.

Alternatively, remove plants with rhizomes or tubers from their pots, clipping off all remaining roots and foliage, and store each one in its own tightly sealed bag or jar of slightly dampened

Because foliage is going to die back anyway and would foul the water, always give plants that are going to spend the winter outdoors a "haircut" before lowering them back into the water.

peat moss, in a cool, dark place. Don't forget to label!

Tropical Waterlilies and Tropical Marginals

These plants will not survive the winter outdoors in most parts of North America. Some water gardeners find it simplest to haul them out after they've finished blooming and discard them (on the compost pile, never in a natural or man-made waterway). They then clean the pots and save them for re-use next spring, when they buy new plants. If you consider this wasteful, you can try your hand at overwintering the plants indoors.

A tropical waterlily tuber will survive the winter easily if you keep it in a plastic baggie of slightly damp sand.

Here's a quick method for overwintering indoors, especially good for waterlilies.

You will need clean glass jars or plastic baggies, labels, and damp sand (builder's sand or "sandbox" sand).

1. Remove leaves and roots so just the tubers or rootstocks are left; rinse off as much dirt/mud as possible. (Note that some potbound tropical waterlilies may have produced "baby" tubers, which are the ones you want; the larger, grape- to walnut-sized "mother tuber" has probably exhausted itself and can be discarded.)
2. Float them in tepid water for a day or two. Viable ones will sink, and spoiled ones will float (toss out the spoiled ones). To ensure complete dormancy, some experts advise leaving the viable ones in water for up to two weeks, rinsing them daily. Others suggest air-drying them for a few days in a cool, dry room. Both techniques work well.
3. Then place the tubers or rootstocks in a glass jar or plastic bag of barely damp sand, label, and store in a cool, dry, nonfreezing place.

You can also keep the plants going all winter in an aquarium, which is especially good for smaller aquatic plants. You will have to maintain a fairly high water temperature, at least 75 degrees F, and provide abundant fluorescent lighting. The best place for such a setup is a good-sized, heated greenhouse, though there are water gardeners who have successfully converted a room or basement to this use. Just cut them back and set the pots in the warm water (replenish the gravel layer on the top of the soil if necessary so you don't muddy your aquarium water).

In addition, many tropical marginals can be overwintered indoors in a sunny window, the houseplant method, which is especially good for papyrus, taro, and the like. Make sure they're pest-free, and set them in a saucer of water that you keep replenished as needed.

Floaters and Submerged Plants

If you don't want to haul out and discard these prolific plants and start with fresh ones next spring, save a few indoors in a warm aquarium, as described above.

Winter Monitoring

No matter what you decide to do with your plants for the winter, realize that despite your best efforts, you may lose a few. This is normal and to be expected. However, as your water-gardening skills and knowledge increase from one year to the next, you'll have many more successes than failures.

For plants stored outdoors in the pool: Do not let the pool freeze solid; keep an open area or gently poke a hole to allow gases to escape.

For plants stored indoors: Check on them every now and then, looking and/or sniffing for rot. Discard obviously rotten plants immediately. If their storage medium (builder's sand or peat moss) seems too dry, moisten lightly.

Aquarium-kept plants just need the water to stay warm and the light from overhead fluorescents to be consistent. If some yellow or die or others grow too rampantly, simply discard them.

Your Pool in Winter

For gardeners in areas with cold and snowy winters, the main worry is the formation of ice on the pond, or worse, that it will freeze solid. If this is a concern for you, you should lower the water level a few inches to a foot (depending on the depth of your pond) in the fall to allow for expanding ice.

A layer of ice on the surface of your pond is bad news. For starters, it prevents the healthy and necessary exchange of

Freezing temperatures can cause problems for your pond's plants and fish unless you take precautions.

gases between the atmosphere and the water. Organic matter trapped in the water will break down and produce foul-smelling toxic gases (ammonia, hydrogen sulfide, and excessive carbon dioxide). Also, an ice layer traps snow on the surface, and even a thin layer prevents sunlight from reaching any plants left to overwinter below. Excessive ice can also damage a pond's liner. (See Pool Aerating Options, below, for ways to keep ice from completely covering your water garden.)

A loose or tented plastic covering can help keep your pond from freezing.

If your pool has a recirculating pump or fountain, you might be tempted to use it to keep water moving all winter and thus prevent ice from forming, or at least forming a permanent cover. But this isn't wise. It may keep the oxygen moving, but it will also send chilly water down to the pool bottom, disturbing and perhaps harming your plants or fish there. Also, it may be meant to be stored (out of the frozen pond) until spring; check the box it came in or contact the manufacturer.

Spring Start-up

The first and most important piece of springtime water-gardening advice is: Wait...don't jump the gun! That is, don't be impatient and get started too

POOL AERATING OPTIONS

- Float a piece of firewood, chunk of scrap wood, ball, or styrofoam in the pond.

- Poke in a pole or branch of some kind, and trek out to the water garden every few days to jiggle it. *Never* bang on the ice to break it; this can injure your fish.

- Set a hot kettle or pan of hot water on the ice to melt it (tie a string to it so you can retrieve it if you're not there when it sinks).

- Buy a pond de-icer, available from water-garden suppliers; this keeps a hole open.

- Buy a stock-tank heater, the kind farmers and ranchers use to keep livestock water troughs free of ice in the winter months. (These come equipped with a thermostat and turn on when the water temperature drops below freezing.)

- In mild climates, you may construct a simple plastic tent over the water garden and let heat escape on days when it builds up. (Cut slits in the plastic to accomplish this.)

TAKE INVENTORY

One thing you can do early in the gardening year is to take stock of what you have on hand and what you need to buy.

- **Check on plants you've stored to see how they've fared.** Discard rhizomes and tubers that show signs of rot or mold. Brush the straw off the surface of sheared, potted plants and nudge around for signs of life. But don't make hasty decisions about viability—a plant that looks dead could actually just be dormant.

- **Order new plants now!** Water-garden catalogs start appearing in mailboxes in early spring, or you can make a visit to their websites and see what will be offered this year (see the listings on page 168). If you have certain special plants in mind, it's best to order them sooner rather than later, so

the supplier doesn't run out and you have to settle for a substitute or refund. Don't worry about receiving an order too early—specialty nurseries monitor the weather conditions in every Hardiness Zone and don't ship until it's safe and until the proper planting time.

- **Determine which supplies you are going to need.** Some large pots or tubs? Fertilizer tablets? A patch kit for the pool liner, just in case? Maybe some new water-garden statuary or a fountain? New fish? Filter pads? Extra neutralizer tablets to treat chlorinated water or chloramines-treated water (they're always handy for emergencies)?

early. If the air, and most importantly, the water, hasn't warmed up sufficiently, the plants won't grow and indeed may suffer a setback. While hardy waterlilies and other hardy aquatics tolerate water temperatures in the 50s, tropical plants won't be able to get going until it's in the 70s (which, in some areas, may not be until early June).

Note: For details on planting various water-garden plants for the first time, please consult Chapter 2.

Reviving Tropical Waterlilies

If they were overwintered indoors, check on the tubers a few weeks before your last expected frost date. Are sprouts emerging?

If they are, pot them temporarily in 5- or 6-inch pots of heavy garden soil, about a quarter-inch deep. Top the pot with rinsed pebbles, stick in a label—making sure to keep the growing points clear—then set them in a bucket of warm water or an aquarium. (You may need to add an aquarium heater in order to maintain a water temperature of 70 to 80 degrees F.) Shine grow lights or fluorescent lights over this temporary home.

If new sprouts are not emerging, place the tubers in water on a sunny windowsill to get them going. Then follow the directions above.

On transplanting day, be sure the pool temperature has climbed into the 70s. Repot each tuber into a large container of heavy garden soil, fertilize, and top with a layer of rinsed gravel. Then carefully lower the pot into the pool to a depth of no more than 6 to 8 inches below the water surface, using supports if you need them. You'll be delighted at how fast overwintered lilies surge into new growth and are soon producing new blossoms!

Spring is the perfect time to divide and replant because everything is poised to burst into vigorous new growth.

Reviving Hardy Waterlilies and Lotus

If they were overwintered indoors, check potted ones for signs of life and wait till you see some new growth before doing anything. Then, fertilize and top off with rinsed fresh gravel if necessary. Take them outdoors and give them a good soaking with the hose (taking care not to wash away their soil). After excess water has drained away, return them to the pool. (If you overwintered their rootstocks in jars or baggies, wait until the water has warmed up enough outdoors before repotting and returning them to the pool as described above—and remember to handle them with great care.)

If they were overwintered in the pool, then on one fine day in spring, when the water temperature is in the 50s, don your waders and retrieve the pots. Haul them out of the pool and examine them carefully for signs of life—they should be just breaking dormancy. Remove any bedraggled foliage that may be just hanging on. Then, poke in some fertilizer, replenish the gravel layer if need be, and return the plants to the water, immersing them no more than 6 to 8 inches (use supports to lift them higher). In the ensuing weeks, watch for, first, new leaves and, soon after, the first new buds and blossoms. (Second-year lotuses have a good chance of blooming at last!)

Marginals in Spring

If they were overwintered indoors, follow the same procedure as you would for reviving overwintered hardy waterlilies. Return them to the pool when the water temperature is at least in the 50s, and give them the shallow water they prefer.

If they were overwintered in the pool, you might find, to your chagrin, that you've lost a plant or two to rot—the best way to avoid disappointing losses is not to delay retrieving them; when the water warms up, get to work! Follow the same steps you would for reviving hardy waterlilies, but when you return the pots to the pool, immerse them only about 2 inches below the water surface (a shelf or support will be necessary).

Dividing Aquatic Plants

Spring is the perfect time to divide and replant because everything is poised to burst into vigorous new growth. For hardy

Carefully lower a potted waterlily back into the water so the protective layer of gravel doesn't spill off. This layer keeps the soil from fouling the water and prevents fish from dislodging a plant.

plants, including hardy waterlilies and water-loving irises, wait until the water temperature is at least in the 50s. For tropical plants, including tropical waterlilies, act when the water temperatures are consistently in the mid-70s.

1. Wash off the dirt from the rootstock of the plant you wish to divide. Then gently probe it, looking for growing tips.

2. Cut it into chunks with a sharp, clean knife, making sure that each piece has at least one growing tip evident, plus some viable roots (often white, but sometimes brown or reddish). It may take more than a knife blade to split up some rootbound hardy marginals—the sharp edge of a trowel or shovel may be necessary.

3. Repot according to the directions in Chapter 2. Don't forget to fertilize and, if you wish, label each plant.

4. Place hardy aquatics right in the water, at the proper depths, assuming the water temperature is right. Tender and tropical plants may be held indoors in a bucket of warm water or a heated aquarium until conditions are warm enough out in the pool.

Use a sharp knife, trowel, or shovel when dividing water plants and make sure each section has some good, viable roots.

You never know who will show up at your pond.

Floaters and Submerged Plants in Spring

Whether you order them or managed to hold some over from last season, these plants are best put into the water when it is warm enough. Follow the same guidelines for their larger companions, that is, hardy ones can go in when the water temperature is at 50 degrees and tropical ones are best held until the water is 70 degrees.

You never need to start with very many of these plants, as they grow lustily and you'll soon have all you need. As ever, excess plants can and should be scooped out periodically and discarded. Toss them on your compost pile or dig them into your garden soil elsewhere in your yard, but never throw them into natural or man-made waterways.

Caring for Fish

Fish are a great joy to have in a water garden; it's fun to observe them, with their bright colors under the water surface. You may have added them for practical reasons as well, for not only are they a reliable source of carbon

A home water garden can be a great environment for fish. Here's what you can do to make it as welcoming as possible:

- **Provide plenty of plant coverage**—remember the two-thirds rule, because the more water surface that is covered by foliage, the more places the fish will have to seek shelter on hot sunny days and hide from predators.

- **Include floating plants,** because fish not only like to hide under them but will lay their eggs in the trailing roots.

- **Include submerged plants** (formerly billed as "oxygenating" plants), which produce valuable oxygen for the pool while the sun shines and filter

excess nutrients. These also may provide shelter and a place to lay eggs.

- **Pool water should be chlorine- and chloramines-free;** chlorine evaporates on its own after a day or two, and chemicals sold by pet stores and water-garden suppliers remove chloramines.

- **Agitate the water** on hot, still nights (with a stick, a running sprinkler, or a fountain) when oxygen levels are otherwise precipitously low.

dioxide (a by-product of their respiration and used by your aquatic plants) but they dine on insect pests (especially mosquito larvae and aphids), algae, and decaying organic material in the water. For more details on choosing and "installing" fish—including calculating how many are appropriate for your water garden—please refer to Chapter 2.

But you cannot simply toss fish into the water and forget about them. They need your attention if they are to remain healthy and to survive from one year to the next.

Feeding Your Fish

With the exception of koi, the truth is that you don't really have to feed a small population of fish. They'll get by just fine on mosquito larvae,

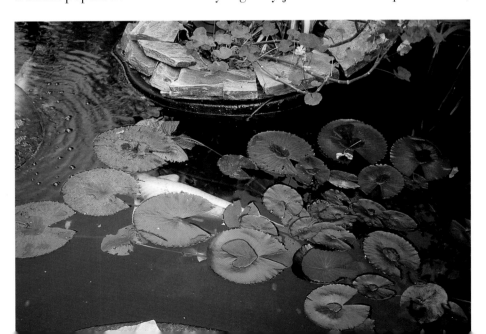

The rule of thumb for feeding fish is never give them more than they can consume in five minutes.

duckweed, and other naturally available food. However, all fish will grow larger and healthier and be more inclined to reproduce, if you supplement their diet.

Feed small fish on flakes, and larger fish on pellets (if in doubt, get instructions from wherever you bought the fish). How much? That will depend on the type of fish, how active they are, and the time of year (or water temperature). The rule of thumb is to give them only what they will consume in five minutes. Uneaten food will foul the water. If your fish are new, feeding them antibiotic food for about ten days will lessen their chances of disease.

Breeding and Spawning

Your fish may reproduce without any intervention from you. As mentioned above, though, extra food early in the season will encourage them—especially the females. If you look closely, you'll be able to tell which fish are female because they will become noticeably fatter. They lay their eggs in submerged plants and the trailing roots of floating plants, and can even be observed inspecting potential sites in advance. As for the males, their behavior, too, will give them away. They'll nudge and chase the females around the pool, sometimes so enthusiastically that you'll see them arching out of the water. When the female is ready, she'll release her eggs at her chosen spot and the male, right behind her, will unleash milt to fertilize them. The fry generally hatch in three to seven days.

Overpopulation

The downside to all the activity and excitement that led to more fish is that sometimes it results in too many. Signs that this is a problem in your pool include murky or even smelly water, overturned and uprooted plants (casualties of their zeal for finding food), and a pump filter that seems to need ever-more-frequent cleaning or changing. Or, due to not enough oxygen, the fish can be seen gasping for air at the water's surface, especially in the early morning.

The solution is obvious—take some out. Don't kill them, feed them to the cat, dump them in a natural or man-made waterway, or flush them down the toilet! There are more merciful alternatives—give them away, or sell them to the local pet shop. Or raise them as pets in a bowl or aquarium.

You can also slow down the reproductive rates of the remaining fish by reducing or withholding fish food.

> *You can also slow down the reproductive rates of the remaining fish by reducing or withholding fish food.*

Surviving Winter

In late summer and autumn, feed your fish regularly so they head into this time with reserves of fat (high-carbohydrate food is ideal)—stop when the water temperatures drop into the low 50s. The fish will naturally slow down as the water temperature gets colder. Eventually, they retreat to the muck at the bottom of the pool and enter a hibernation-like state. In the coldest zones, and if the pool is shallow, fish (especially fancy, expensive koi) might need to be brought inside for the winter, though even in Zone 4 fish can stay in their outdoor home if it is 30 to 48 inches deep and you use a de-icer.

If an ice layer should form during the winter, always remove it because if the pool's surface freezes solid, toxic gases may get trapped and the fish will be killed. Maintain an opening, so the water remains oxygenated. If you poke through the ice with a branch or stick, avoid stirring up the bottom of the pool; if you disturb the fish, they'll expend valuable energy.

Early Spring Care

On one of your early-season visits out to the pool, you may notice that the fish are in motion again. You may be tempted to feed them as soon as you see them—don't. Wait until the water temperatures rise about 50 degrees F. (the water will warm up more slowly than the air). If you feed your fish too early, and the temperatures take a dip, they won't be able to finish digesting, which is harmful. A stressed fish is more vulnerable to disease. As the water temperature rises, reintroduce food gradually. It is always better to underfeed than overfeed at this point.

Why Fish Die

Assuming your fish came to you in good health, the only explanation for early death is stress. Fish experience stress if you place them in water that is too cold or water that contains chlorine or chloramines; these problems are preventable. Exposed fish may languish and die immediately, or the stress to their systems may make them sick and they'll die of one of the many diseases that afflict fish. So if you are topping off your pool with hose water, hang around and monitor the job—if you wander off or leave the house,

CAN'T MISS TIP:

HELPING BABY FISH

New baby fish can look quite different from their parents. You might even mistake them for mosquito larvae wiggling around, but they'll grow quickly, especially if you toss in a little flake food for them. As with all little creatures in nature, the road to adulthood is not easy for new little fish, or "fry." They are easy targets for visiting birds. They might even be eaten by adult fish! Good plant cover in your pool will give them a fighting chance, but if you are concerned about their survival, you can net them and raise them elsewhere.

you may forget to shut it off, which results in too much cold water and/or too much chloramines entering the pool.

Low oxygen levels are a leading cause of fish death. You'll see them gasping at the water's surface. If you've been less than observant, you'll step out one morning, too late, and find their little bodies floating. The biology of a garden pool is such that during the day, when the sun is shining, the plants are producing oxygen and consuming carbon dioxide (part of the photosynthesis process), while the animals (fish in particular) are producing carbon dioxide and consuming oxygen. This cycle comes to a halt at nightfall (no sunlight means no photosynthesis). Help your fish by keeping the pool's oxygen levels up: Grow plenty of submerged plants, and run a fountain, waterfall, or close-by sprinkler on hot, muggy nights. Otherwise, churn the water with a bit of hose spray or even a stick before you go to bed. And pray for rain, which eases this problem naturally.

Although this pond is larger than most backyard water gardens, you can see what happens when algae takes over!

Fish Diseases and Treatments

Try to catch an afflicted fish and inspect it carefully. Certain fungal organisms cause sores, a cloudy film over the eyes, or rotting tails and fins. Parasites may cover the body, evident as small red or white spots. Luckily, all of these woes, if caught in time, are treatable. Remedies are sold wherever fish are sold, in the form of liquids you can add to the pool water. Always follow label directions exactly.

Coping with Water-Quality Issues

Nothing makes a new water gardener fret more than the clarity of the pool's water. But, as explained in Chapter 2, unlike a backyard swimming pool, a healthy home water garden is *never* perfectly clear, nor is it meant to be. Duckweed or other floating plants may proliferate, algae will be present, and fish will contribute waste. The goal is to manage your little ecosystem so water quality does not become a problem. If you've planned and planted carefully, more than likely your pool will be just fine. A small amount of algae, visible as a slightly green or bronze cast to the water and as a coating that forms on the sides, is both normal and healthy. The key to water clarity is plenty of submerged plants and a few fish.

TOOLS FOR REMOVING ALGAE

You can use your bare hands if you wish, but the following items will also extract algae from the water:

• a long stick or broom handle

• a net

• a toilet bowl brush

• an "algae twister" gadget, a long stick with two sharp-toothed metal circles at the end

• a small, thin-tined rake (a gardening tool for children)

You don't have to use a fancy tool to remove excess algae. A toilet bowl brush works just fine!

Always dispose of algae properly by digging it into a garden bed elsewhere in your yard or adding it to the compost pile—*do not* dump it in natural or man-made waterways, where it can grow to become a bigger problem.

Realize that physically removing algae from your pool is a temporary solution. It will make your display look better for a while, but if you don't address the cause of the bloom, more will grow to replace that which you have extracted.

Algae Matters

WHEN YOUR WATER GARDEN IS FIRST INSTALLED: New water gardens inevitably experience a flush of algal growth, called a "bloom." This is because there is plenty of light available to encourage its growth and dissolved minerals in the pool water to nourish it. Small or shallow pools and container gardens are most vulnerable because they heat up faster—and algae love very warm water. It's easy to panic, and tempting to scoop out the gobs of algae or empty the pool entirely. The best policy, though, is to wait it out. Once your plants get established and start to cover the water surface and the pool settles down into a state of balance, the algae *will* dissipate.

TYPES OF ALGAE: The botanical identity of algae may not interest you when it is the enemy, but close observation will reveal that there are indeed different kinds. Some are stringy, some float on the surface, some are unicellular and suspended in the water. They can be green, reddish, or brownish. All reproduce amazingly fast.

WHEN THE PROBLEM PERSISTS: If your pool is not newly installed and appears overwhelmed with a smelly pea soup of algae, you have a problem—and you have options. As mentioned above, repeatedly extracting algae or

TROUBLE-SHOOTING ALGAE PROBLEMS

Condition: Extra nutrients

If you've been overfertilizing your aquatic plants, perhaps excess nutrients have been leaching into the water and nourishing the growth of algae. Fertilizer runoff from your lawn or surrounding garden can also contribute to the problem.

Strategies:

- Cut back on plant food, both amount and frequency, and see if that helps, particularly during hot weather.

- Divert runoff away from your water garden. Bank up the sides better, or make channels to direct the flow of water away from the pool.

- Keep yellowing and dying foliage trimmed off.

- Cover the pond with netting during autumn, to catch falling leaves.

Condition: High water temperature

Algae thrive in very warm water. Several long, hot sunny days can sometimes start up an algae problem for the first time. Shallow water, along the pool edge and especially if your pool has a shelf, is especially prone to overheating.

Strategies:

- Add more plants. A healthy pool should have two-thirds of its surface covered with plants. Waterlilies will give you a lot of bang for your buck. And floating plants are also a smart addition because they will out-compete the algae for minerals dissolved in the water.

- Cool the water. Provide some extra shade, especially over the shelf area. A large beach umbrella over the water in the hottest part of the day just might do the trick.

Condition: Fish food

Overfeeding your fish can lead to an algae problem. The food that they don't eat will break down in the water, adding to the organic broth. Fish excrement and its by-product ammonia also encourage the growth of algae.

Strategies:

- Never feed your fish more than they can consume in a five-minute period.

- Feed them even less if algal growth is a chronic problem.

- Take out some fish . . . there may be too many (consult Chapter 2 to figure out how many fish your pool can support).

- Install a filter that removes fish waste (see Chapter 2 for a description of the various options; your best bet, but possibly the most expensive, is a biological filter).

- Treat the water with a liquid "ammonia-remover" chemical (one popular brand name is Ammo-Lock™), which is available from water-garden suppliers. Read the label and follow the directions to the letter, particularly regarding how much to use for the size of your pool.

- Add bacteria (available at water-garden suppliers) to more quickly break down fish by-products.

Condition: Improper pH level

The ideal level is between 6.5 and 8.5, for the health of your plants and fish; around 7.0 is considered ideal. The most common algae seen in home water gardens are green algae, which thrives in more alkaline water. Reddish algae prefer more acidic water.

Strategies:

- Invest in a simple pH test kit to determine your pool's pH level. The best time to check is first thing in the morning.

- Adjust the pH to a better level with the addition of special liquid pool chemicals, available where the test kit and other water-garden supplies are sold; there are "pH-up" and "pH-down" products, so make sure you get the right one. Then follow the directions on the label exactly.

emptying and refilling the pool won't solve anything, unless you discover and address what caused the excessive growth in the first place. See Troubleshooting Algae Problems, above.

Additional Water Treatments to Consider

When you are fretting about poor water clarity in your pool and unwanted algae, you have additional options for addressing the problem. Just remember, whatever you do, try one remedy at a time to see whether it is effective. And if you invest in chemical treatments, read the labels carefully to find out if they will harm your fish or snail population (perhaps you can remove them temporarily)—and always follow dose instructions and application advice to the letter. Note that repeated treatments are sometimes necessary.

If a treatment kills algae in the pool, you'll want to remove the algae as quickly as possible. Otherwise, it will rot in place, generating more nutrients and continuing your water-quality problems.

Blue dye darkens the water and deprives algae of the light it needs to grow.

FILTERS: Mechanical filters strain algae and other particles before they break down into algae food. A biological filter will do an even better job, removing some or all of the algae's food sources from the water—but it can be more expensive. (For more details on filters, see Chapter 2.)

MOVING WATER: This is debatable for deterring algae. A pump, fountain, or waterfall aerates your pool water, bringing in more oxygen. While this is essential for healthy bacteria levels (which create a balanced pond with clearer water), too much turbulence stirs up mineral-rich sediment from the bottom of the pool and delivers it to the light and warmth of the upper water layers—thus fueling continuous production of algae.

WATER DYES: Pools with few plants, which therefore lack sufficient plant coverage, are especially vulnerable to algal blooms. Water dyes darken the water, depriving algae of the light it needs to grow and prosper. The dyes create an inky, mirror-like surface that fades over time and will need occasional replenishing.

UV LIGHTS: In recent years, these have become more popular. The latest trend is to include them with filters. They are effective at killing free-floating algae, in particular.

STRAW: A "natural" remedy that has received attention in recent years. Its algae-thwarting properties were discovered by accident when a British farmer noticed that algae disappeared from a pond on his property after some bales of hay fell into the water. It doesn't actually kill algae—it prevents it from growing, especially if the water garden has a good supply of oxygen.

At any rate, since then, researchers have established that barley straw is the most effective algae deterrent, and wheat straw runs a close second.

Apply twice a year, once in autumn and again in spring, before algae growth has a chance to ramp up. Not much straw is required—about 2 pounds, bundled so it will be easier to recover, treats a 3-foot-deep pool that measures about 20 by 50 feet; if your pool is smaller, even less will do the job.

CREATURES THAT EAT ALGAE: Your fish will eat some algae, but if you really want to target the green stuff, try water fleas (*Daphnia*). Actually crustaceans, these little creatures will consume nothing but algae. You can find them at pet shops that have fish supplies. Warning: If you have fish in your pool, these tasty little fellows may not live long enough to do their job.

Another option is freshwater snails. These graze small amounts of algae from the sides of the pool and eat pond detritus before it breaks down into nutrients. Again, they are available wherever water-garden or aquarium supplies are sold. (Make sure you get the right ones—not the varieties that dine on plants!)

When Bottom Waste Accumulates

Over time, your pool may gradually gain a layer of muck and silt on the bottom. It is composed of fish and snail waste, decayed plant material, dead leaves, and other solids that may have settled out.

Beneficial bacteria lodge in this layer and break down the organic matter into gases such as ammonia. Algae will consume some ammonia, as will your waterlilies and other pool plants. But if it builds up too much or is too rich, your water will become cloudy, smelly, and algae-laden.

If you decide you need to take action, just remember not to be overzealous and remove all of the muck. A certain amount of bottom muck is fine, indeed good, for your pool's ecosystem. A layer an inch or two thick is tolerable. A good rule of thumb is to take out only about 70 percent of the offending material at any one time.

Here, then, are your options:

■ Add bacteria to speed up the breakdown of the organic matter. Water-garden suppliers offer these in both liquid and powdered forms.

■ Scoop out some of the silt occasionally, especially during the height of the growing season when it is at its thickest. But be careful—a sharp-edged tool such as a shovel can nick or tear your liner, which leads to even bigger problems! A plastic bucket or scoop, or even your bare hands, would be better.

A certain amount of bottom muck is fine, indeed good, for your pool's ecosystem. A layer an inch or two thick is tolerable. A good rule of thumb is to take out only about 70 percent of the offending material at any one time.

THE BIG CLEANUP

A water garden that enjoys regular maintenance does not need to be drained and refilled. If it has a proper balance of plants and creatures and has reached a state of equilibrium where algae (though present) are not out of control, leave well enough alone. Introducing a fresh batch of water to a pool returns it to "square one."

That said, there may be times when this onerous chore becomes necessary. You should proceed with the empty-and-refill, regardless of the timing, if the water doesn't clear and appears to be getting worse, or if the pool develops an ongoing problem with oily scum on the surface (this is often accompanied by an unpleasant smell).

A dry day in fall is generally preferable over spring for an empty-and-refill. Because the temperatures are dropping and the days are getting shorter, your plants are on their way to dormancy and your fish are slowing down—so the whole operation will be less traumatic for them. Plus the water isn't as cold in fall as in early spring for you to be working in it.

- Remove all the plants.
- Catch as many fish and snails as you can, which is easier once the water level has been lowered significantly. Hold them in buckets of *pond* water in a shady place. Segregate them in separate buckets so they'll get enough oxygen, and so they aren't tempted to eat each other in the confined space.
- Remove the water. Don't divert the water into the street .(This may be illegal in your area.) Use it for watering other parts of your yard.
- Don't scrub! Leave a little because, over time, beneficial bacteria have established themselves in the muck and it's unwise to remove them.
- Refill. Let the water stand for a few days so the remaining silt can settle on the bottom and so any chlorine can dissipate. (Treat the water if it has chloramines.)
- Meanwhile, check on the reserved plants and creatures daily to make sure they are not suffering.
- Return the plants to the pool at their proper depths, on shelves or with supports as necessary.

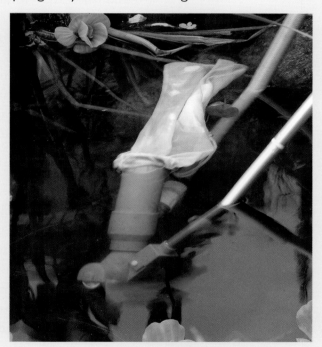

Catalogs and nurseries sell a variety of equipment to help you clean your water garden.

■ Invest in a "pond-sweep" vacuuming tool and use it monthly during the growing season. Follow the manufacturer's operating instructions and advice for best results.

■ Completely empty the pool, remove most of the muck, and refill. This is a drastic step, best done for older ponds that have accumulated a thick layer over several years. See The Big Cleanup, page 109, for details. *Tip:* Dispose of organically rich muck elsewhere in your yard or on your compost pile.

Water Loss

Even though home water gardens are contained environments, they do still lose water sometimes. Assuming that your pool liner was intact at installation, and installed "on the level" (see Chapter 1 for more details on this important issue), water loss is rarely a major problem. However, it happens, and there are several things you can do.

Topping Off

All water gardens lose some water due to evaporation, most rapidly during hot spells. Keep an eye on the situation and intervene when the water level drops more than an inch or so—you'll see the high-water line on the side of your pool. Don't delay—or the remedy becomes more complicated and time-consuming (see The Big Cleanup, page 109).

When it's time to replenish some lost water ("top off"), make sure that your plants will not be disturbed and that the pool adjusts gradually to the addition of water of a different temperature. Chlorine present in the added water should not pose a problem, and it will evaporate away in a day or two. (Interestingly, studies have shown that such a small amount may have value as a fungicide and algicide.) A nominal amount of chloramines-treated water shouldn't be a big deal either, but you can combat its effects if you feel it's warranted by adding a neutralizer (see Chapter 1 for more information).

You have two choices for adding water: the hose and a sprinkler. Whatever you decide, you must check often and turn off the water when the former water level is achieved. Otherwise, your fish could get a lethal dose of chlorine or chloramines and die. Stay around—check over the pool and all its contents, or putter in the vicinity. Or set a timer to remind yourself.

Keep an eye on your pond so that you never have to add more than an inch or two of water at a time. Yes, tap water contains chlorine and possibly chloramines, but adding small amounts won't cause a problem for your fish or plants.

THE GARDEN HOSE: Gently trickle the water into the pool. Never lower the end into the pool—the water won't get aerated and the low oxygen levels are bad for your fish. Plus you might leave it too long and the pool might overflow and/or your fish might die from too much chlorine or chloramines entering their world. Either stand (or sit) there, or prop it up so it splashes in, perhaps off to one side.

AN OVERHEAD SPRINKLER: Set it close to the pool's edge and run it on low. This way, water will softly rain down on the water's surface and gradually raise the water level.

A Damaged Pool

You don't want all the time, effort, and money you invested in installing your pool to go to waste by having a damaged liner. Luckily, there are ways to cope with this possibility.

PREVENTATIVE MEASURES: Here's how to protect your pool's liner from any chance of damage:

- Cover the edges the pool when you install it (so its edges are not exposed to sunlight).
- Repair minor problems immediately when spotted.
- Keep it filled.
- If you notice animal pests, don't procrastinate in dealing with them, as they may get bolder and more destructive with each successive visit. (Their antics, or claws, can cause scratches and tears.) For advice on chasing them away, see page 114 later in this chapter.

PROBLEM: You should suspect that your liner is damaged when the water level drops very quickly and without warning. A pool liner can sustain damage in various ways: from the sharp nails of a marauding animal, from a lash from an errant string trimmer, from a lawn mower that strayed too close, or from the natural decomposition process that occurs when the plastic has been exposed to sunlight for too long.

DIAGNOSIS: To get a good look at the problem, lower the water level gradually. Do this either by bailing or siphoning. When you spot the damaged area, stop. If the damage is in the lower part of the pool and you need to remove a large amount of the pool's water, you may have to take out some or all of the plants and fish and hold them in buckets of pond water until the problem is fixed.

CAN'T MISS TIP:

ADDING MORE WATER

If you waited too long and your pool turns out to need the addition of several inches of water, you need to be more cautious. Otherwise, your fish may suffer shock or an overdose of chlorine or chloramines. Also, a sudden dose of cold water can force some plants, tropical waterlilies, in particular, into premature dormancy and cause hardy ones to become deformed. Here's what to do:

- Top off the pool a little bit each day, for several days, according to the directions at left.

- Reserve sufficient water in buckets for a few days, treating for chloramines or letting chlorine evaporate, *then* add their contents in batches.

Do not replace more than 10 to 20 percent of a pool's water at any one time.

PATCHING LEAKS IN FLEXIBLE LINERS

Pinholes and nicks are not a crisis and can easily be repaired. A dab of neoprene paint or duct tape—applied to a dry area—may be sufficient (but will need to be renewed every now and then). Larger cuts require a patch (PVC or EPDM); kits are available from catalogs and garden centers that sell liners and cater to water gardening. They include the patch itself, some adhesive material, and instructions for use.

To get the longest possible life out of a patch, follow these instructions to the letter.

1. Do the repair on a warm, sunny day when the liner will be most flexible.

2. Scrub the trouble spot clean (free of algae and all other residue).

3. Apply the patch only to a totally dry, prepared area. Be generous: Use a patch at least 2 inches longer and 2 inches wider than the gash or hole.

4. As you work, take care not to stretch the liner, as this can weaken the result.

5. Once the patch is in place, let it dry completely before refilling the pool. (If you are impatient, you may direct hot air from a blow drier to ensure a tight seal and that the patch is snug. WARNING: Be extra-cautious about running the hair dryer or any electrical appliance near water—do not stand in or even touch the water while operating it!)

Repair leaks as you find them. The proper materials are available wherever liners are sold.

TREATMENT: If it's a minor leak, you can repair it with a patch (see Patching Leaks in Flexible Liners, above). If you find extensive tearing or cracking, unfortunately it may be time to replace the liner.

EXCESSIVE WATER LOSS: If you are unlucky enough to be away from home for some time when a leak occurs, don't panic on your return. All may not be lost, as nature has its own survival mechanisms.

Take out the plants and prune off all the obviously dead growth. You may notice that the stress caused leaves to die; new growth will be poised to sprout when the plant recovers. You may also notice that algae is coating the plants, staving off dehydration—imagine, being grateful for algae!

Next, move the plants to containers of water that have sat long enough for the chlorine to evaporate or to water that has been treated.

As for any fish or snails, they will have retreated to the area with the most water or plant cover to protect themselves from drying out. If the pool is really low, feel around in the silt at the pool's bottom. Transfer survivors to a temporary home. You may lose a few more, but some may pull through.

Then, clean out all dead plant debris and dead creatures before repairing the leak and refilling the pool. Remember, as always, to let the water warm up for a day or two and to let the chlorine dissipate (or treat it for chloramines). Then, get the survivors back into the pool as quickly as possible.

Stormy Weather

Bad weather can wreak havoc on your yard in general, your water garden included. Wait until it passes before going outside to assess the damage and clean up. In particular, you don't want to be outdoors during an electrical storm, as water is an excellent conductor of lightning and you would be in grave danger.

When it's safe, the first order of business is tidying up. Right toppled plants and garden ornaments. Remove debris that landed in the pool. Shore up eroded pondside berms and replace damaged pondside landscaping.

Run-off

Post-storm, your pool will have gained not only water but also dirt and even pollutants (such as oil from a nearby road or garden chemicals—fertilizer as well as weed-killers).

If the water's merely muddy, wait. The silt should settle in a few hours or a day. At that point, if it's excessive, you can scoop or siphon some out (thus temporarily re-muddying the water) and get rid of it.

If you suspect substances in the runoff will harm your plants or fish (or a few days have gone by and they are showing signs of damage), you may need to intervene. Emptying and refilling the entire pool is a drastic step and may not be necessary. Instead, take out the potted plants and leach them—water thoroughly with a hose. Then return them to the pool. Fish can be quarantined for a few days (in pool water or buckets of freshly treated water). Then lower the pool's water level and add fresh water, according to the directions on page 110, Topping Off. If there still seems to be a problem, you might indeed have to empty and refill the pool.

Hail

These little balls of ice are a by-product of summer storms, when precipitation high in the atmosphere forms into small, roundish, layered lumps

during its descent. Hail usually starts and stops suddenly, but even a brief shower of hail can wreak havoc in a water garden. The relatively thin, horizontal lilypads are especially vulnerable—hail shreds and perforates them. There's little you can do except prune off the damage and wait for the plants to rebound—which won't take long.

Dealing with Water-Garden Pests

Water gardens are irresistible to a number of animals—you may be delighted to see birds, butterflies, dragonflies, even an occasional frog or turtle. But not all visitors are welcome. In the case of wild animals, they may be drawn to our yards because their own habitat is shrinking or there are few natural predators left to check their populations. Trapping and releasing these visitors in a faraway area is now illegal in many places, as is killing them with poison or a gun. Check with your local animal-control officer for advice and help.

As when coping with pests in other parts of your home landscape, sometimes a balance can be struck . . . a "truce" if you will. You may be able to tolerate the presence of an occasional visitor without going to war. But if an uninvited animal becomes a major threat to the beauty and health of your water garden, there are steps you can take to discourage it. Admittedly, some of these techniques are homegrown, but they may work well for you.

A hungry heron can do a lot of damage in a short period of time.

Above all, keep a sharp lookout. Catch the culprit in the act or observe it from indoors, so you know who your enemy is!

Birds

HERONS: Of all the birds drawn to water gardens, these are the most destructive. Most common are blue herons. They tend to travel alone and have excellent eyesight, and they can zero in on even a small water garden. They

SIX DEFENSIVE STRATEGIES FOR A PEST-FREE WATER GARDEN

Bear in mind that most unwelcome visitors are waders, not swimmers—so take steps to discourage them if you're in an area where they are likely to be a problem.

1. **No side shelves.** A shelf on the side of a garden pool is a wonderful platform from which animals can fish, nibble on plants, or step down into the depths of the pool. A straight-sided pond is a great deterrent for keeping out marauders like raccoons.

2. If you have side shelves, or even if you don't, **keep lots of potted marginals along the sides** of your display, allowing no corridor or opening. The same goes for pondside landscaping.

3. **Spread a thin net or grate** across the entire pool, anchoring it firmly to the banks. (Water-garden suppliers offer types that are relatively unobtrusive-looking.)

4. **Put a pile of rocks or a few cinderblocks on the bottom** of the pond to give fish a place to retreat.

5. **Place a decoy** in the garden—an owl, a snake, even a fake alligator. What kind will depend on what kind of pest you are combating (see Herons above, for instance).

6. **String fishing line around the edges** of the pond, fastened to sticks or plants. While not completely invisible, it's not that obtrusive and it can thwart pests (mammals as well as birds) who approach the water garden on foot.

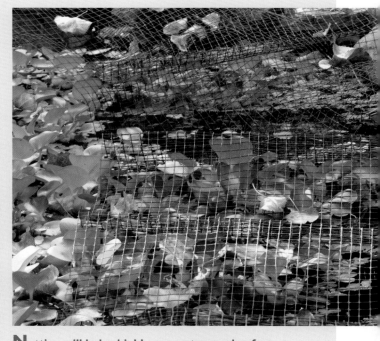

Netting will help shield your water garden from predators. (It's also useful for catching falling leaves in autumn.)

immediately begin dining on your fish—their long legs and long, sharp beaks make them fast, versatile fishermen. A single bird can empty an entire pool in short order.

STRATEGIES:

■ Erect a system of fishing lines around the pool's perimeter to trip them up as they fly in or walk up to your water garden's edge. Be thorough, as a bird may retreat only to return and try approaching from another angle.

■ Put a heron-shaped decoy in your pool. Because herons are territorial, the one flying by may decide your water garden is "taken." Move the decoy around from time to time so any real heron watching doesn't begin to suspect the truth.

■ Employ decoy or "scare" balloons that vegetable gardeners sometimes use to discourage marauding crows.

■ Use a Scarecrow™, which is a motion sensor attached to a sprinkler head. It shoots off a spray of water to scare off intruders.

■ Put in one or several baby floating alligators (the plastic kind, of course!).

DUCKS AND GEESE: These creatures go after your aquatic plants, especially the submerged ones and newly planted waterlilies. Ducks also really like *Sagittaria*—indeed, one of its common names is "duck potato." They will

This pond is protected by netting.

sometimes eat pieces out of
mature lilypads, too. Their
droppings can become a problem
in the pool (excessive organic
matter leads to algal blooms) as
well as on the ground nearby (an
unsightly, smelly mess). They
may also carry diseases that can
transfer to your fish.

STRATEGIES:

■ Make sure your pool has
the recommended two-thirds
plant coverage over the water
surface—there will be less
space for ducks or geese to
occupy/work with/swim in.

■ Noise-making repellents
are sometimes effective,
including scare balloons and a small transistor radio tuned to a
talk station.

■ Animals, decoy or otherwise—especially a dog in the yard—are often
effective deterrents.

■ Plant thickly around the edges of your water garden, especially tall
or substantial plants. (The drawback to this tack, of course, is that you
may not be able to see into the pool so well.)

■ Grape Koolaid™ powder sprinkled around the edge of the pond is
said to deter geese. Apparently they don't like the smell!

A raised water garden close to
the house may attract fewer
unwanted visitors.

Mammals

RACCOONS: These marauding pests adore water. They're expert fishermen,
but aren't very graceful, which means that in their zeal for a meal, they'll
knock over pots and the supports or nudge roots or plant tags out of place.
They may go after your fish and freshwater snails.

STRATEGIES:

■ Provide your fish with plentiful places to hide—remember the two-
thirds plant coverage recommendation.

■ Never add crawfish to a water garden; raccoons find these totally
irresistible.

■ Plant a forest of marginals inside the pool near the edges as well as on the adjacent dry land to thwart their passage into the water. (Again, this is a trade-off, for you end up blocking a good view of your display. Try wispier or shorter ones first; they may just do the trick.)

■ Use light, sound, or noise repellents. Scarecrow™, a motion sensor attached to a sprinkler head, shoots a spray of water to scare off intruders.

■ Sprinkle blood meal around the perimeter of the pool and replenish it periodically . . . apparently raccoons abhor the smell.

■ Install a thin-wire electrical fence, a safe distance back from the water's edge.

MUSKRATS: These creatures can become a problem if a wild wetland, pond, or stream is not far from your house. They like to dine on arrowhead, cattails, grasses, reeds, and sedges, and they find waterlily and canna rootstocks a gourmet treat. Like raccoons, they are clumsy—they can knock over plants, supports, and water-garden statuary. Also their sharp claws can slash a plastic liner. One visit, and your water garden will be a real mess.

STRATEGIES:

■ Try any of the tactics listed above for discouraging raccoons.

■ Muskrats especially like to nibble on grassy-leaved marginals, in the water or on the banks, so avoid those and grow more substantial or broad-leaved choices.

■ Erect a small, low fence around your pool.

CATS: Domestic cats are often enthralled by water gardens, but don't seem as willing as wild animals to climb in after the fish. A cat is more likely

Cats are endlessly fascinated by fish in water gardens but aren't usually willing to get wet.

Turtles may find your water garden, but they usually don't damage it.

Sometimes a turtle finds your water garden and you are enchanted to see it there, probably on a rock sunning itself. For the most part, turtles are vegetarians and just one is unlikely to cause any problems. However, if you notice your waterlilies are being nibbled on more than you'd like or if there's a significant drop in your fish population, a turtle, or more than one, could be the culprit.

The only remedy is to capture it and return it to its natural habitat, which is probably nearby—unlike trapping, say, a large mammal like a muskrat, this tack is generally not illegal (though you can check with your local animal control officer to be sure). Netting a turtle, however, is easier said than done. They are not as slow moving as children's stories would have you believe—when in the water. Your best bet is to catch it when it is sunning itself, usually in the morning. (Turtles are cold-blooded and must sit in the sun to raise their body temperature.)

If your problem is a large and scary-looking snapping turtle, be careful! If you're strong and brave, handle it by a back leg to avoid the reach of its jaws. To lure it into a trap in the water, use oily canned sardines or a piece of chicken liver as bait. If the project is too daunting, call your local anima control officer or wildlife service for help.

to just sit watching at the pool's edge for hours. Take care not to startle it, though, or it might take a tumble into the pool—this is most likely to happen in the case of a container water garden, where the fascinated feline may keep a precarious perch on the rim.

STRATEGIES:

■ Try a bad-smelling repellent, and replenish occasionally, especially after a rain. Possibilities include liquid from boiled onions, hot pepper sauce, and commercially available cat repellents.

■ Lay lengths of poultry/chicken wire around your water garden, projecting about a foot from the edge. If this area is not given over to grass, you may be able to hide it from view with a thin layer of soil or mulch. When a cat walks on it or tries to dig, its paws get snagged and it decides to go elsewhere.

■ Install a sensor that shoots a jet of water, at regular intervals or when it detects motion nearby—this often deters cats.

Insect Pests and Diseases

A healthy water garden rarely has problems. But if yours does, here are some common culprits and strategies for combating them. Incidentally, every time you "top off" your pool is an opportunity to check over the plants with care—it's a good idea to hang around the area while the water level is being replenished anyway.

APHIDS: The same tiny, busy white or black pests that afflict some plants out in your main garden may also descend upon your water garden. If left unchecked, they soon cover their victims, thanks to their fast reproduction rate and voracious appetite.

STRATEGIES:

■ Be vigilant for these pests and act early, and you may beat them back.

■ Remove and discard affected leaves.

■ Push affected leaves and flower buds under the water and swish around to dislodge the aphids—your fish will then eat them.

■ Use a blast from the hose to get them off—your fish will then eat them.

This lilypad has been dinner for China mark moth larvae.

■ Immerse an entire plant temporarily, for a day or so. The aphids will let go and float to the water surface, where you can skim them off.

■ As extra insurance, use the fall cleanup time as an opportunity to tidy up afflicted plants. Note that a cold winter will kill any lingering aphids.

CHEWING INSECTS: From leafminers to Japanese beetles, the foliage of water-garden plants may be subject to small or big nibbling problems. Observe carefully so you can find and identify the culprit correctly.

STRATEGIES:

■ Keep yellowing and dying leaves trimmed off, so pests don't have a place to hide.

■ If there are only a few, handpick and destroy individual insects.

■ Remove and discard affected leaves.

■ Use an insecticide only if the problem is severe, and be sure to get professional advice on the correct product and the correct application of it. (Some products are harmful to fish or even illegal to use in water.) Bt and neem-based repellents may be suitable and safe.

■ Handpick the offending bugs and drown them in a bucket of soapy water. (Do not squish them—though you may feel full of revenge, this actually releases their pheremones, which may attract even more to your yard!)

CHINA MARK MOTH LARVAE: Adult *Hydrocampa* moths lay their eggs on the undersides of lilypads. These hatch as small green or yellowish leaf-cutting larvae. They don't actually eat your aquatic plants' leaves—rather, they build themselves little floats that hide them from predators, then sail around in your pool dining on small bits of organic matter. When they are ready to pupate, they drill a hole into a waterlily leaf stem and emerge later

If your water garden is located away from the house, you should be extra-vigilant. Insect and disease damage can occur very quickly.

as adult moths, completing their life cycle. Meanwhile, the affected leaf suffers from this intrusion, usually turning limp or yellow and eventually dying.

STRATEGIES:

■ During the summer months, wipe off the bottoms of your lilypads to dislodge egg masses.

■ If you spot the larvae, handpick and dispose of them far from the pool.

■ Pick off—right at the plant's crown—and dispose of leaves whose stems have been affected.

■ For large infestations, a dusting of Bti powder *(Bacillus thuringiensis israelensis)* may be effective. This treatment will not harm your fish.

MOSQUITOES: From spring to summer, mosquitoes begin breeding in any open water they can find, leading to an infestation later in the summer. Always an annoyance, mosquitoes can also be dangerous; they are capable of transferring diseases to humans, including the West Nile virus. Their eggs hatch in water gardens and the larvae can grow to maturity there.

STRATEGIES:

■ Eliminate all other possible breeding spots in your yard, including puddles and water accumulated in buckets, pots, or discarded tires.

■ Keep fish—and feed them a bit less, so they'll be eager to dine on mosquito larvae.

■ Buy and toss in Mosquito Dunks, donut-shaped tablets with Bt in them that kill the larvae but do not harm pond life. One dunk will treat 100 square feet of (surface) water; you can break dunks into smaller pieces for smaller ponds or container gardens.

CROWN OR ROOT ROT: This is a disease of some hardy waterlily rootstocks and, unfortunately, highly contagious from one plant to the next. Early signs include rotting, black stems; buds that never quite make it to the water's surface, turning black, rotting, and falling away; lilypads that start out fine but for no apparent reason turn yellow and die after a few days; and an odd, unpleasant smell. Close inspection of the plant may reveal an alarming sight: The tuber or rhizome may be coated in gelatinous, foul-smelling goo.

Older Marliacea varieties of waterlilies and some in the yellow-to-orange range are especially susceptible and pass their vulnerability on to their offspring. Examples include: 'Paul Hariot', 'Gloriosa', and 'Sunrise'.

STRATEGIES:

■ Soak all newly arrived rootstocks overnight in a bucket of water to which you have added a few drops of fungicide, then pot up in a clean pot.

■ Haul affected plants out of the pool immediately upon detection of this problem.

■ Unpot them, wash off the rhizome or tuber, and inspect. If they are rotten through and through, discard them and the soil they were growing in. If there appear to be some healthy parts, chop off all the bad parts and repot the good parts in new soil and clean gravel and hope for the best.

■ When re-using pots that had affected plants, be sure to wash out and disinfect the pot (with a mild bleach solution) first.

■ A fungicide, applied early, might be effective in slowing or halting the disease. But some fungicides are toxic to fish, so read the labels carefully for this warning.

LEAF SPOT: Suspect a fungal problem when you see little brown spots on the leaves of your aquatic plants, or browned edges. Hot and humid weather seems to exacerbate these problems. Prolonged rainy spells can also bring on an outbreak.

Clean your filter regularly for the health of your water garden.

■ Remove and discard affected foliage right at the plant's crown. (It will soon generate replacement leaves.)

■ Quarantine or remove affected plants and treat with a fungicide. But read the label carefully, not only to get the exact application instructions, but also to find out if the fungicide might harm your fish.

Equipment Maintenance

Equipment in a water garden is optional, but can be nice to have. A pump and/or filter will circulate your water, helping to keep it aerated, cleaner, and healthier for both fish and plants, and it can power a fountain, stream flow, or tumbling waterfall.

Getting the proper-capacity equipment for your water garden in the first place will go a long way towards keeping maintenance as hassle-free as possible. You need to know your pond's capacity at the outset and make an appropriate match (for instance, a filter's package will state "for ponds up to 400 gallons"). Basic shopping and installation issues for pond equipment are addressed, as are important safety features, in Chapter 2.

Whenever you buy equipment for your water garden, always save the packaging and the manual or instructions that came with it. This material can help answer your questions about it long after the item has been installed. You can also check back with the store or catalog where you bought it and/or the person you hired to put it in place.

There are general maintenance issues that come up over the course of the gardening year, all easily dealt with. Of course, on the off chance that an unexpected problem develops, such as damage to your equipment or its electrical cords,

Be sure to clear the pump in your fountain from time to time.

shut down the power immediately and get professional help; replacement equipment may be needed.

Pumps

KEEP IT CLEAN: Some pumps have inlet screens; some of the newer models come with sponges that trap sediment so it can't get inside your pump. These protective devices need to be rinsed regularly and replaced from time to time. Instructions come with the pump.

KEEP THE LINES CLEAR: Most pumps are served by sturdy, flexible black plastic tubing. Clogs and kinks can occur every now and then; your best defense is to check on the tubing occasionally to confirm that nothing is amiss, and straighten it out if need be. To address a suspected or confirmed clog, turn off the pump first, then follow the manufacturer's directions for flushing the line.

Filters

Over time, a filter becomes clogged with pond debris, dirt, and bits of algae. Depending on the type of filter, you must then either remove and replace the filter with a new, clean one, or rinse or backwash the existing one. (Some filters may have a drain valve in the bottom where you can release the accumulated gunk.) In larger pools with lots of plants and fish, during the height of the season, this procedure may be necessary on a daily or weekly basis for mechanical filters, four times a month for biological filters. Directions come with your filter; follow them carefully so you don't damage your filter and so you get peak performance out of it.

POOL EQUIPMENT IN WINTER

If you live where winters are mild, you can leave a pump in the water. Indeed, a circulating pump is nice to have because it keeps the water moving and thus aerated. As a result (if this is a concern), ice is less likely to form. You ought to raise it up off the pool floor on some sort of platform or support, though, so it doesn't send moving water down to the very bottom where plants and fish may be at rest.

If your winters are fairly cold, however, it's wise to disconnect and remove the filter and the pump. Drain and clean them, then store them indoors. Drain all pipes so they can't freeze and crack.

Can't Miss
Water Garden
Favorites

Water-gardening in a milder climate—that is, within USDA Zones 6-10—turns out to be both easy and a joy. Many aquatic plants are sun-lovers, relish warm water, and tolerate humidity well, so they grow readily and bloom enthusiastically. You can and should site your display to maximize these good growing conditions. (See Chapter 1 for details.)

A long growing season is another plus. Depending on where you live, you can enjoy your water-garden display for between six and ten, or even more, months. There will still be some winter "down time," in which the plants slow down and bloom less or stop blooming. This is your opportunity to prune, to reduce or cease fertilizing, to let your fish rest, to perform routine

The owner's personality is evident in this pond, even though it began as a pre-formed liner.

KEY TO ICONS

Along with each plant entry, you will notice small graphic icons. They convey additional useful information about the plant's characteristics or benefits. There are also icons indicating light requirements.

🦋	attracts butterflies	🌼	long bloom period
🐦	attracts hummingbirds	Ⓝ	native plant
🍐	produces edible plant parts	🐝	supports bees
🧴	has fragrance	🪺	provides food or shelter for wildlife
🍒	produces attractive fruit	💐	good for containers
💐	suitable for cut flowers	🏆	award winner

☀️	full sun	☀️	part shade
☀️	part sun	☀️	full shade

maintenance on your pump and/or filter, and to clean up around the pond. If there's any risk of freezing temperatures, you may overwinter precious plants indoors. Please consult Chapter 3 for more details on these projects and their timing. Spring, when the water temperatures rise again, will bring you and your plants a fresh start.

In this chapter, you will find helpful profiles of your choices, from tropical and hardy waterlilies to lotuses to marginals to floaters and submerged plants. Obviously, this is but a sampling of all that the water-garden-plant world has to offer. But the ones included here are special. To assure your gardening success, they have been tried and tested, passing muster on the following key criteria:

- beautiful flowers
- dependable performance
- easy care
- wide availability

So the following entries are intended to get you started, to guide you in your choices—and to inspire you. Have fun choosing and shopping for the ones that appeal to you, and be open to making changes or exploring further options in the future. This directory is simply meant to open the garden gate and welcome you into the delightful world of water gardening.

A Glossary of Water-Gardening Terms

Some of the following entries include terms that may be unfamiliar to you, but are in common use not only in water-gardening books, but at nurseries and in catalog descriptions as well.

Aeration: the process of splashing or agitating still water to add oxygen
Algal bloom: a sudden, rapid growth of algae
Algicide: a chemical that controls or kills algae in your water garden
Anther: often borne at the top of the stamen, the pollen-bearing part
Backfill: the process of scooping or shoveling soil back into a pot or hole
Berm: a raised barrier or small hill, usually earthen
Biological filter: a device that uses beneficial bacteria to convert organic pollutants (from fish waste, mostly) into relatively harmless substances
Bog plant: used by many water-garden catalogs to mean the same thing as marginal or emergent plant (although true bog plants are habitat-specific and thus may have special soil, pH, and exposure requirements)

Chlorine: used by municipalities to treat water so it will be safe for drinking; harmful to fish—however, it dissipates if the water sits for a day or two

Chloramines: used by municipalities to treat water so it will be safe for drinking; a mix of chlorine and ammonia; can only be neutralized with chemicals (is toxic to fish)

Crown: the point where stems emerge from the root system

Cultivar: short for "cultivated variety," an improved/altered version of a plant species

Emergent: also called a marginal plant; a plant that thrives in wet soil or shallow water

Filter plant: an aquatic plant, usually a marginal or floater, that gets its nutrition from your pool's water, thus reducing the amount available to pesky algae and therefore contributing to clearer water

Floater: a plant whose leaves float on the surface, with roots trailing below and deriving nutrition from the water

Fry: baby fish

GFCI/GFI: ground fault circuit interrupter, an important safety device that instantly turns off power if moisture gets into electrical wiring associated with a water display

Hardscape: any landscaping material that is not plants—e.g. stones, statuary, edging materials

Hardy waterlily: a waterlily that grows from a rhizome and is generally considered hardy in USDA Zones 3-10; the flowers are usually smaller than those of tropical waterlilies and float on the water's surface

Have fun choosing and shopping for the plants that appeal to you, and be open to making changes or exploring further options in the future.

WHEN TO PLANT

Here are some general guidelines for when it ought to be safe to introduce plants to your display, which may be altered by local weather conditions from one year to the next. When in doubt, check with another local water gardener, the nearest water-garden center, or members of a regional water-garden or pond society.

Please note that in the warmest areas of Florida and the Gulf Coast, you can plant at almost any time and the plants will reach full, enjoyable size that same season.

- **ZONE 6:** mid- to late May
- **ZONE 7:** late April to May
- **ZONE 8:** mid-April
- **ZONE 9:** mid-March to early April
- **ZONE 10:** March to early April

COMMON MISTAKES TO AVOID

Sometimes beginning water gardeners, despite their best intentions, do something they shouldn't and their displays run into trouble or don't look as good as possible. Luckily, common mistakes are easily avoided. Look to the main chapters for more detailed explanations, but here's what not to do.

- **Do not site the water garden in a secluded or shady spot.** Water plants need lots of sunshine in order to thrive and produce flowers. Also, debris from trees and shrubs (fallen leaves, twigs, etc.) are a hassle to keep dredging out of the water. Plus the roots of trees and shrubs will interfere with the pool—indeed, you may find it nearly impossible to dig a nice, smooth, sufficiently deep hole in such a spot. The exception is that aboveground displays that include a fountain and/or shade-tolerant plants may be situated in a secluded spot, but you will have to keep an eye on things to make sure debris doesn't accumulate.

- **Do not be too quick to empty and refill the display.** Some people do this when they observe algae accumulating—and they panic. But tap water (hose water) has been treated with chemicals, principally chlorine and/or chloramines, which can harm fish. Plus the introduction of cold water will be a shock to your recently introduced plants. Algae build-up in the early days is actually perfectly normal; it will subside when the pool reaches a state of balance and plants are covering around two-thirds of the water's surface . . . so be patient and don't interfere!

- **Do not scrub algae off the sides.** A coating of algae forms naturally over time along the sides of your display, whether an in-ground pool or a tub garden. It is not harmful and, indeed, becomes part of the water garden's ecosystem. Scrubbing it or swiping at it only dislodges the algae and clouds the water.

- **Do not plant too soon.** If you place pots of plants in the water when it's too cold, they may struggle, be shocked into dormancy, or even die. Hardy plants may go in after the water temperature has reached at least 50 degrees F; tropicals, including tropical waterlilies, must wait until it's 70 degrees F.

- **Do not plant too deeply.** Potted waterlilies can be placed in deeper water, 18 to 24 inches down, but everything else (marginals and submerged plants) is best in shallow water, at most only 6 inches deep. Some are fine with only an inch of water over their pot's surface.

- **Do not overplant.** When there are too many plants in your display, growth becomes stunted or distorted and the plants may not flower as well as they should. Leaves can rear up out of the water (called "pyramiding"), which looks bad and is bad for the plants. Coverage of about two-thirds of the water surface is healthiest and considered ideal because then you can also see some reflection in the water. A packed pool just looks like an overgrown swamp. Always plan for a plant's "mature size" (which is noted in the plant descriptions that follow).

- **Do not overfeed fish.** Never feed your fish more than they can consume in about five minutes. Uneaten food breaks down and makes the water murky, providing food/fuel for algal growth. And overfed fish make more waste, which also clouds the water, creates a bad smell, and overburdens your filter.

Head: a term used for pumps—refers to the vertical distance between the pump itself and the water outlet

Koi: large ornamental carp popular with water gardeners

Liner: any plastic or fiberglass material used to line a hole in the ground to form a pool or water display

Marginal: also called an emergent plant; a plant that thrives in wet soil or shallow water

Oxygenator: a plant that produces oxygen from its submerged foliage; also called a submerged plant

Pondscaping: an industry term meaning landscaping in and around a garden pool

Rhizome: a rootstock—technically, an underground, horizontally-growing stem

Runoff: unwanted water, or dirt or debris-filled water, that enters a water display

Sepal: One of the outer whorl of protective leaf-like structures that clasp a flowerbud and splay outward and down when the flower opens

Spitter: a small ornamental fountain that emits a small spray of water

Stamen: the pollen-filled anther plus a filament holding it up; very prominent in waterlilies; the male part of the plant

Submerged plant: a plant that survives and grows with most of its mass underwater; an oxygenator

Tropical waterlily: a waterlily that grows from a small, roundish tuber; the flowers are usually larger than those of hardies and are often held above the water's surface; does best in warm climates but may be grown elsewhere provided the water is at least 70 degrees F. and there's plenty of warm sunshine

Tuber: a thick underground storage organ that includes growing points or eyes

Underlayment: special durable fabric that is placed in a hole before the liner, to protect the liner from punctures or damage from below

Viviparous: when small "baby plants" form on the leaves of a mature plant

There's a lot going on in this water garden, but it all looks great together.

Tropical
Waterlilies

Spectacularly beautiful and justly popular in mild growing climates, tropical waterlilies are often the crown jewel of a pond or container display. The large flowers of the day-bloomers generally open mid-morning and close by late afternoon, offering plentiful prime-time viewing. Those of the night-bloomers tend to unfurl late in the day and stay open all night, closing the following morning; this makes them a great choice for busy people who are away all day at school or work and want to savor their water garden in the evening hours. For everyone else, one or two of these beauties extends your pleasure around the clock!

Tropical waterlily flowers generally last for about three or four days. You'll also notice that they tend to proudly raise their blossoms up above the water's surface by several inches, and often have a sweet, enticing fragrance.

Full sun is important for best bloom, though some waterlilies will manage with less. (Those that can are so noted in the entries that follow.) For best results, gardeners need to supply warm water (in the 70s, at least) and maximum sun exposure. In settings with blazing summer sun, a little shade relief at midday, either from adjacent plants or an umbrella, might be desirable.

Both tropical and hardy waterlilies can live outside in the pool all winter long in USDA Zones 9 and 10, during which time they'll continue blooming, though not as heavily—as you might expect.

For Zones 8 and colder, all waterlilies must be either treated as (expensive!) annuals (taken out of the water and discarded) or overwintered inside. For overwintering techniques, consult Chapter 3, starting on page 93.

Note: If you don't know your USDA Hardiness Zone, find your location on the map on page 166.

Albert Greenberg
***Nymphaea* 'Albert Greenberg'**
FLOWER COLOR: "sunset"
MATURE FLOWER SIZE: 6-7 inches across
BLOOM TIME: summer
MATURE PLANT SPREAD: 5-8 square feet
LEAF COLOR: green speckled with purple

This is an excellent and very popular "sunset" colored, free-flowering waterlily. Distinctive cup-shaped blooms waft a lovely, sweet scent. Petals are yellow to light orange, with melon-pink tips—like a tropical fruit punch. They are a striking contrast to the purple-splashed lilypads.

This robust tropical is a good choice for medium to large pools, but it will adapt to life in a large container, just grow more compactly. It tolerates less than full sun, still blooming lustily. 'Albert Greenberg' can be a long bloomer, even in cooler zones.

Antares
***Nymphaea* 'Antares'**
FLOWER COLOR: red
MATURE FLOWER SIZE: 6-10 inches across
BLOOM TIME: summer
MATURE PLANT SPREAD: 5-7 square feet
LEAF COLOR: dark bronze to dark green

This is one of the finest night-bloomers, which means it opens in late afternoon and stays on display well into the following morning. Spectacular, large cuplike blooms sport deep magenta petals and orange stamens—wow! These rise well above the water surface and are complemented by the undulated, round leaves that start out bronze and mature to apple green (with brown undersides); the contrast with the flowers is superb in either stage of leaf development. The flowers also have a strong scent.

This beauty grows best in medium to large pools.

Dauben
Nymphaea 'Dauben'
FLOWER COLOR: light blue
MATURE FLOWER SIZE: 4-6 inches across
BLOOM TIME: summer
MATURE PLANT SPREAD: 2-7 square feet
LEAF COLOR: green

An enduringly popular dwarf-sized waterlily, 'Dauben' (syn. 'Daubeniana') is both pretty and prolific. The small, pale blue flowers fit in well with other-color waterlilies and many marginals. Flowers open early and stay open until dusk. Thanks to the plant's overall smaller size and tendency to bloom continuously, it's great for container displays and also works in a shallow pond, under only 4 inches of water. It has a strong, pleasantly sweet scent.

It is also highly viviparous. Baby leaves forming on individual lilypads can develop into small plants! In a container setting, it might be advisable to remove the "babies" so the display doesn't get too crowded. Either discard them or grow new plants according to the instructions in Chapter 2.

Though it thrives in heat, like other viviparous blue and purple waterlilies, 'Dauben' also seems to tolerate colder water temperatures than other tropicals, and may be left in the pool all winter if no freeze is expected. It prefers a bright location but will flower with only three to four hours of sun.

Director George T. Moore
Nymphaea 'Director George T. Moore'
FLOWER COLOR: violet-blue
MATURE FLOWER SIZE: 7-10 inches across
BLOOM TIME: summer
MATURE PLANT SPREAD: 5-8 square feet
LEAF COLOR: green with some purple markings

The big draw for this waterlily is the unusually deep flower color—it's a dark, rich violet, beautiful with a gold center and purple stamens. After the first day, it opens nice and wide to a distinctive star shape. It also wafts a sweet scent. An established plant blooms prolifically.

'Director George T. Moore' (syn. 'Director Moore') is a fine choice for medium and larger pools, though it will also remain compact in a container garden. It will prosper even with some shade or reduced hours of sunlight.

Emily Grant Hutchings

Nymphaea 'Emily Grant Hutchings'

FLOWER COLOR: pink
MATURE FLOWER SIZE: 6-8 inches across
BLOOM TIME: summer
MATURE PLANT SPREAD: 6-7 square feet
LEAF COLOR: bronze-green

A luscious night-bloomer! The petals are hot, rosy pink, the anthers orange-pink, and the stamens ruby-red. The flowers are cup-shaped and large, and radiate a soft, lovely scent. Against the backdrop of handsome bronze-green leaves, these glorious flowers are quite impressive. Enjoy the blossoms from late afternoon and into the following morning.

'Emily Grant Hutchings' also tends to start blooming earlier in the season than other night-bloomers, so you can enjoy it over a longer period. It is a fairly expansive plant, however, and is best in medium to large pool displays.

Evelyn Randig

Nymphaea 'Evelyn Randig'

FLOWER COLOR: pink
MATURE FLOWER SIZE: 7-9 inches across
BLOOM TIME: summer
MATURE PLANT SPREAD: 5-7 square feet
LEAF COLOR: green with dark blotches

Gorgeous is the word for this beauty! The large blossoms start out in a cuplike shape, becoming more open and star-like over the ensuing days. And the color is fabulous, featuring deep, intense, raspberry-pink petals that contrast with sparkling golden stamens. These make quite a show among the purple- to chocolate-splashed lilypads. (Fragrance is slight, but present—and is more noticeable in bouquets brought indoors.)

'Evelyn Randig' is a dramatic choice for medium and large pools.

TROPICAL WATERLILIES

General Pershing
Nymphaea 'General Pershing'
FLOWER COLOR: lavender-pink
MATURE FLOWER SIZE: 8-11 inches across
BLOOM TIME: summer
MATURE PLANT SPREAD: 6-8 square feet
LEAF COLOR: olive green with purple markings

Though in commerce since 1920, this old-timer continues to be popular and thus widely available, and no wonder. Its spectacular flowers are really big, particularly in comparison to the smaller, roundish lilypads and less sprawling plant size. Starting out cup-shaped, they gradually splay outward until they are more flat. Very double, orchid pink, and sweetly fragrant, they're beautiful to behold. The flower bud is also lovely—green with magenta stripes. The blooms open early and stay open until twilight.

This waterlily is suitable for most any size pool but is too big for a container.

Josephine
Nymphaea 'Josephine'
FLOWER COLOR: white
MATURE FLOWER SIZE: 3-4 inches across
BLOOM TIME: summer
MATURE PLANT SPREAD: 2-4 square feet
LEAF COLOR: green

Sweet scent and cuplike, crisp white blossoms make this waterlily a real prize—it's certainly a superior among small whites. It blooms continuously, making it a satisfying choice for beginning water gardeners seeking a dependable plant, as well as for more experienced gardeners who appreciate its prolific nature.

Thanks to its smaller flowers and smaller spread, 'Josephine' is a fine choice for smaller water gardens and containers.

Madame Ganna Walska
Nymphaea 'Ganna Walska'
FLOWER COLOR: lavender
MATURE FLOWER SIZE: 4-6 inches across
BLOOM TIME: summer
MATURE PLANT SPREAD: 3-7 square feet
LEAF COLOR: green with light red markings

Miami Rose
Nymphaea 'Miami Rose'
FLOWER COLOR: pink
MATURE FLOWER SIZE: 4-6 inches across
BLOOM TIME: summer
MATURE PLANT SPREAD: 4-5 square feet
LEAF COLOR: dark green splashed with burgundy

A lovely, vivacious pastel flower—it is lavender (with hints of pink), with golden stamens. The inner petals and stamens are especially bright. 'Madame Ganna Walska' looks wonderful in the company of other purple or pink waterlilies, tying the display together. It is very easy to grow and blooms profusely.

As for the foliage, it is light green but splashed and marked with wine-red. The pads are also highly viviparous. Overall, the plant seems to be more cold-tolerant than other tropicals.

This splendid waterlily was named after the original owner/creator of Lotusland, a celebrated garden near Santa Barbara, California, that features many exotically beautiful plants.

What makes these beautiful, full-petaled flowers especially unique is their starry shape, rising well above the water's surface and drawing plenty of admiration. The color is quite a rich, raspberry pink, and the blossoms waft a lovely fragrance. They look sensational against the burgundy-splashed leaves.

'Miami Rose' may be grown in medium-sized pools, but will also adapt to smaller ones or even a large container.

TROPICAL WATERLILIES

Panama Pacific
Nymphaea 'Panama Pacific'

FLOWER COLOR: purple
MATURE FLOWER SIZE: 4-6 inches across
BLOOM TIME: summer
MATURE PLANT SPREAD: 5-7 square feet
LEAF COLOR: green with maroon mottling

Very reliable, and very beautiful. The petals are vividly plum-purple, the stamens yellow, and the yellow anthers are purple-tipped—wow! The fragrance is especially sweet and intense. Once established, flowers are produced almost continuously, and they make a great bouquet choice, too.

For a tropical, 'Panama Pacific' is fairly cold-hardy, so even in Zones 6 and 7, you can enjoy it over a long period. Lots of young plants are produced viviparously on the pads. The lilypads are somewhat smaller than many waterlilies.

This is an outstanding choice for any size pool and adapts to life in a large container. It also tolerates less sun and cooler temperatures better than most and is undemanding.

Queen of Siam
Nymphaea 'Queen of Siam'

FLOWER COLOR: pink
MATURE FLOWER SIZE: 4-6 inches across
BLOOM TIME: summer
MATURE PLANT SPREAD: 4-6 square feet
LEAF COLOR: green with plentiful purple markings

One of the best newer varieties, 'Queen of Siam' features lovely, raspberry-pink petals that are yellow at the base, plus yellow stamens—a flower at its peak looks lit from within! The heavily mottled leaves are always attractive and make a striking backdrop. They are viviparous.

This fine waterlily is ideal for medium-sized pools. It's more compact than the somewhat similar 'Evelyn Randig' and even tolerates less sun or part-day shade.

Red Flare
Nymphaea 'Red Flare'
FLOWER COLOR: red
MATURE FLOWER SIZE: 7-10 inches across
BLOOM TIME: summer
MATURE PLANT SPREAD: 5-6 square feet
LEAF COLOR: maroon

This popular night-bloomer is aptly named. The flowers may be held an entire foot above the water's surface and are a splendid, rich red that is slow to fade. Though not very intense, a sweet fragrance is definitely present.

Coupled with the maroon, serrated leaves, these dark red flowers are magnificent. Maroon stamens are a nice match for the foliage. Be sure to display this one where it can be appreciated often; it shows up well with night lighting (see Chapter 1).

'Red Flare' will prosper in any size of pool, but is at its best in medium to large ones.

St. Louis Gold
Nymphaea 'St. Louis Gold'
FLOWER COLOR: deep yellow
MATURE FLOWER SIZE: 5-6 inches across
BLOOM TIME: summer
MATURE PLANT SPREAD: 5-7 square feet
LEAF COLOR: olive green

An old favorite, 'St. Louis Gold' has admirably stood the test of time. Valued for its rich yellow coloration and free-flowering habit, its flowers open late and close late.

New leaves tend to be bronze-colored with purple blotches, but these soon mature to olive green. At any stage, they flatter the abundant golden flowers.

Thanks to its smaller leaf spread, 'St. Louis Gold' can be grown in medium to smaller pools, but will grow smaller in a container display.

TROPICAL WATERLILIES

Teri Dunn
Nymphaea 'Teri Dunn'
FLOWER COLOR: blue
MATURE FLOWER SIZE: 4-6 inches across
BLOOM TIME: summer
MATURE PLANT SPREAD: 3-5 square feet
LEAF COLOR: medium green

A nice, relatively new blue introduction that is being praised for its manageable plant size, eager flowering, and viviparous qualities. The flower is a pretty, sky blue centered with yellow. It's a good companion for darker-hued waterlilies, from purple to pink, and also holds it own quite well grown solo in a large container.

This waterlily was developed from *Nymphaea colorata*, the same species that is also the parent of the darker-hued 'Director George T. Moore', and it shares with that sibling an ability to tolerate cooler water temperatures. However, it is a smaller-sized plant, able to prosper in a smaller pool or, as mentioned above, a container display.

Texas Shell Pink
Nymphaea 'Texas Shell Pink'
FLOWER COLOR: creamy pink
MATURE FLOWER SIZE: 6-8 inches across
BLOOM TIME: summer
MATURE PLANT SPREAD: 5-7 square feet
LEAF COLOR: dark yellow-green

Almost two-toned, the spectacular blossoms of night-blooming 'Texas Shell Pink' feature reddish sepals to the outside and red-tipped, creamy white petals within; the stamens are yellow. This coloration shows off to good advantage at twilight, when the flowers really seem to glow. The fragrance is rather spicy and has been likened to cinnamon.

A big, free-flowering plant, 'Texas Shell Pink' is best grown in a medium or large pool.

Tina

Nymphaea 'Tina'

FLOWER COLOR: purple
MATURE FLOWER SIZE: 4-6 inches across
BLOOM TIME: summer
MATURE PLANT SPREAD: 3-5 square feet
LEAF COLOR: medium green

Cuplike flowers radiating a sweet, enticing fragrance appear in great numbers. The flower is a bit unusual, in that it has fewer petals than most, but the intense color still commands plenty of attention—it's a deep, rich, royal blue-purple, which contrasts nicely with the gold center and lavender stamens. The solid green leaves are quite viviparous.

Because the plant is relatively compact, it may be grown very well in a container. It's also a fine choice for small to medium pool displays.

Wood's White Knight

Nymphaea 'Wood's White Knight'

FLOWER COLOR: white
MATURE FLOWER SIZE: 10-12 inches across
BLOOM TIME: summer
MATURE PLANT SPREAD: 8-10 square feet
LEAF COLOR: medium green

A big, bold night-bloomer, 'Wood's White Knight' has creamy white flowers so full of petals that they almost remind you of a plush peony blossom. Blooms are held high out of the water. White stamens are yellow tipped. The fragrance is rich and sweet and wafts over the garden on warm evenings. Leaves have attractive scalloped edges.

Because it is a sprawling grower, this one is best displayed in a medium to large pool.

Hardy
Waterlilies

The pretty blossoms of "hardies," as these waterlilies are often called, are open most of the day. Although understandably the waterlily of choice in cooler zones, some do fine throughout the country. (Technically, they are considered suitable for USDA Zones 3 to 10.)

The flowers are generally smaller than those of tropicals, and usually float on the water's surface. (For more differences, read the comparison on page 71 of Chapter 2.) Hardies also extend the waterlily color range into red and orange, though these hues can bleach out if they are exposed to prolonged hot sun and high humidity. That said, here are cultivars that have proven to be excellent performers in Zones 6 to 10.

Charles de Meurville
Nymphaea 'Charles de Meurville'
FLOWER COLOR: pink
MATURE FLOWER SIZE: 6-7 inches across
BLOOM TIME: summer
MATURE PLANT SPREAD: 4-7 square feet
LEAF COLOR: dark green

Stunning! Star-shaped fragrant blossoms, large for a hardy waterlily, display a rich range of light and dark pink hues, all centered with brilliant orange stamens. Against the oversized, especially dark, mint-green lilypads, they are really impressive.

For best performance, place 'Charles de Meurville' in a medium- to large-sized pool. You'll discover, to your delight, that it grows quickly. It is among the first to start producing blooms each spring and will continue well into fall.

Chromatella
Nymphaea 'Chromatella'
FLOWER COLOR: yellow
MATURE FLOWER SIZE: 4-6 inches across
BLOOM TIME: summer
MATURE PLANT SPREAD: 3-6 square feet
LEAF COLOR: medium green, blotched purple

Bountiful cuplike blossoms stud the plant from early in the growing season well into the fall months. They are chiffon yellow centered with darker-hued golden yellow stamens and anthers—beautiful! The sweet scent is most pronounced in first-day blooms. Wonderful for bouquets. The flowers also look very grand against the attractive, purple-speckled young foliage (the older foliage is green).

Because *Nymphaea* 'Chromatella' (syn. *Nymphaea* 'Marliacea Chromatella' and *Nymphaea* 'Golden Cup') is relatively small, it is a fine choice for smaller pools and container displays. It tolerates less sun than some of its peers—it will still flower even if it only gets three to four hours a day.

HARDY WATERLILIES

Colorado
Nymphaea 'Colorado'
FLOWER COLOR: pink
MATURE FLOWER SIZE: 4-5 inches across
BLOOM TIME: summer
MATURE PLANT SPREAD: 4-7 square feet
LEAF COLOR: olive to medium green

'Colorado' is a unique color among waterlilies; it is often referred to as apricot or peach but in reality is a classic salmon hue—in fact it is the first salmon pink waterlily to be hybridized. The flower form is star-like, and golden stamens add to the overall glow. The blossoms are produced in great numbers, starting slowly in spring but accelerating as the growing season progresses, and continuing well into fall. Unlike many hardies, it has a pronounced, pleasant scent, and the flowers can extend several inches above the water.

Though not a big or sprawling plant, it does better in a larger pot and a medium- to large-sized pool. It is somewhat shade tolerant.

Escarboucle
Nymphaea 'Escarboucle'
FLOWER COLOR: red
MATURE FLOWER SIZE: 6-7 inches across
BLOOM TIME: summer
MATURE PLANT SPREAD: 4-7 square feet
LEAF COLOR: green

Though this red hardy has been in commerce since 1909, it continues to be very popular. It is beautiful, of course, with its brilliant red petals, the outer ones white-tipped, supported by pink sepals and centered by dark orange stamens; the petals darken richly with each passing day. But that's not all. It's quite prolific, *and* it has a wonderful tendency to keep its flowers open late into the afternoon, significantly later than many of its peers.

However, it is not a small plant. 'Escarboucle' (syn. 'Aflame') is happiest when grown in a medium or large pool. It is also fairly heat tolerant.

James Brydon
Nymphaea 'James Brydon'
FLOWER COLOR: red
MATURE FLOWER SIZE: 4-5 inches across
BLOOM TIME: summer
MATURE PLANT SPREAD: 3-5 square feet
LEAF COLOR: green with purple markings

'James Brydon' is considered by many hobbyists and professionals to be the finest red hardy. It's undeniably gorgeous—each cuplike blossom is plush with ruby red petals, with orangey-red centers that make a brilliant contrast. These waft an enchanting, sweet scent that has been likened to ripe apples.

Meanwhile, the leaves start out a rich shade of purple, eventually gaining more green but retaining some marbling; the stems and leaf undersides remain wine-purple. The overall effect is quite ravishing.

Owing to its smaller spread, 'James Brydon' is appropriate for smaller pools and tub displays, though it will also prosper in a larger water garden. Note that its rhizome is not subject to crown rot—another plus (a previously popular red called 'Gloriosa' was very susceptible). This waterlily does not like high heat and is an especially good choice for cooler climates. It is also more shade tolerant than some.

Joanne Pring
Nymphaea 'Joanne Pring'
FLOWER COLOR: pink
MATURE FLOWER SIZE: 3-4 inches across
BLOOM TIME: summer
MATURE PLANT SPREAD: 3-5 square feet
LEAF COLOR: medium green with purple blotches

This cute little hardy waterlily has two things going for it— it is one of the few pinks that does well in hot, humid climates, and it is small. Its smaller flower and plant size makes it a very nice choice for small ponds as well as container water gardens.

The cuplike flowers of 'Joanne Pring' are produced in abundance. They look especially wonderful with the new foliage, which is bronzy light purple with deep purple patches. Crown rot can be a problem sometimes, so make sure you plant only healthy rhizomes.

HARDY WATERLILIES

Joey Tomocik
Nymphaea 'Joey Tomocik'
FLOWER COLOR: yellow
MATURE FLOWER SIZE: 4-5 inches across
BLOOM TIME: summer
MATURE PLANT SPREAD: 4-5 square feet
LEAF COLOR: medium green

Especially vivid, deep-yellow blooms adorn a medium-sized plant with handsome, nearly round green leaves. Though a hardy, the flowers may stand several inches above the water's surface. They emit a slight spicy fragrance. This is an especially prolific plant—you'll enjoy plenty of blooms. It is a good choice for medium-sized pools.

Dedicated to Joe Tomocik, curator of the water-garden displays at Denver Botanic Gardens and named after his daughter, 'Joey Tomocik' is an International Waterlily and Water Garden Society award winner.

Perry's Baby Red
Nymphaea 'Perry's Baby Red'
FLOWER COLOR: red
MATURE FLOWER SIZE: 3-4 inches across
BLOOM TIME: summer
MATURE PLANT SPREAD: 3-5 square feet
LEAF COLOR: medium green

One of the most widely grown and cherished smaller waterlilies, this handsome plant is distinguished by strikingly beautiful blossoms in great numbers and an easy-going nature. The plush petals of the cup-shaped flowers are deep, rich wine red, with yellow-orange anthers and orange stamens—a knockout blend of bold colors. Provide a little shade in the heat of midday to preserve the flower color. When immature, the leaves of this hardy are purple, presenting an appealing contrast, though later they moderate to medium green.

Because it flowers so profusely and is not a big plant, 'Perry's Baby Red' is a fine candidate for smaller pools and containers.

Perry's Fire Opal
Nymphaea 'Perry's Fire Opal'
FLOWER COLOR: pink
MATURE FLOWER SIZE: 5-6 inches across
BLOOM TIME: summer
MATURE PLANT SPREAD: 5-7 square feet
LEAF COLOR: bronzy green

A triumph! One of the best ever from Perry Slocum, the late great waterlily hybridizer, it was awarded top honors by the International Waterlily and Water Gardening Society in 1990. The full-petaled, peony-shaped blossoms are a very rich deep pink, centered with orange stamens. (For best color, provide a little shade in the heat of the day.) There's also a sweet fragrance. New leaves emerge purple but eventually turn green. Interestingly, the flowers are nearly the same size as the lilypads—the effect is quite impressive.

'Perry's Fire Opal' adapts well to a tub display or small water garden, growing smaller but still blooming well. It also prospers in larger settings. No matter where you grow it, you will be thrilled with the gorgeous flowers and how abundant they are—all summer long.

Texas Dawn
Nymphaea 'Texas Dawn'
FLOWER COLOR: yellow
MATURE FLOWER SIZE: 6-8 inches across
BLOOM TIME: summer
MATURE PLANT SPREAD: 5-7 square feet
LEAF COLOR: green (new leaves speckled purple)

Winner of the International Waterlily and Water Garden Society's top award in 1990, this outstanding waterlily is prized for its excellent blossoms. Though classed as a yellow and considered one of the best yellow hardy waterlilies of all time, the starry flowers of 'Texas Dawn' exhibit some lovely subtlety. The outer petals are blushed with soft pink, and the entire flower is darker and more golden towards the center; inner petals are rich yellow, and anthers and stamens are pure yellow to match. The pink tendency becomes more pronounced later in the season, when temperatures begin to cool. Also, the sepals have a hint of pink. At all times, the large flowers radiate a citrusy fragrance.

Another distinguishing quality of this fine waterlily is the fact that, unlike most hardies, it holds its blooms dramatically above the surface, sometimes up to 10 inches! The plant itself is medium to large and should be grown in a pool that can accommodate its spread.

Lotus

though a lusty grower in the right conditions and considered a perennial plant, lotuses can be tricky to establish and grow well. They absolutely need the warm water and long growing season that mild climates offer. Humidity doesn't deter them. Please note also that they may not bloom their first year, but if you are patient, you'll get those fabulous blooms in the second and subsequent years. For more information, please read "The Lowdown on Lotus" on page 76 in Chapter 2.

Take note: You, too, can succeed with lotus, but be sure your water garden or container is sited for maximum sun exposure and that the water is nice and warm.

No matter where you grow lotus, please don't be overly focused on getting the flowers and seedpods. The leaves are truly magnificent in their own right and a great asset to any aquatic display. Also, if you are growing lotus only for its beautiful leaves, part-day shade is not a problem.

Though tropical in appearance, the lotus is actually a winter-hardy deciduous plant (capable of growing in USDA Zones 4 to 10). If your area experiences cold winter weather, you may treat your lotus like a hardy waterlily plant, protecting the rhizome from freezing. For details, consult Chapter 3.

Note: If you don't know your USDA Hardiness Zone, find your location on the map on page 166.

Baby Doll
Nelumbo 'Baby Doll'
FLOWER COLOR: white
MATURE FLOWER SIZE: 4-6 inches across
BLOOM TIME: summer
MATURE PLANT HEIGHT: 2-2¹/₂ square feet
LEAF SIZE: 9-11 inches

This is the perfect lotus for anyone wishing to raise one in a container; container displays have the added advantage of warmer water (simply because containers heat up so well when out in the hot sunshine). Its cup-shaped blossoms are lovely and not too large—indeed, the whole plant is smaller in scale than its larger cousins. It is also known to bloom prolifically once established (up to a dozen flowers on a single plant at a time!). The attractive seed capsules that follow are light green at first and then dry to brown.

Chawan Basu
Nelumbo 'Chawan Basu'
FLOWER COLOR: white with pink
MATURE FLOWER SIZE: 5-9 inches across
BLOOM TIME: summer
MATURE PLANT HEIGHT: 2-3 square feet
LEAF SIZE: 14-17 inches

One of the smaller lotuses, this adaptable plant can be added to small- or medium-sized pools or even raised in a container. The flowers are gorgeous: ivory white with hot pink margins and veins; the pods that follow are light green. The delicate scent is especially lovely on just-opened blooms.

For best results, submerge the potted plant in about 12 to 15 inches of water. This lotus prospers in more temperate areas; really hot weather, however, may cause the flowers to flag.

Momo Botan
Nelumbo 'Momo Botan'
FLOWER COLOR: pink
MATURE FLOWER SIZE: 5-6 inches across
BLOOM TIME: summer
MATURE PLANT HEIGHT: 2-4 square feet
LEAF SIZE: 12-15 inches

Mrs. Perry D. Slocum
Nelumbo 'Mrs. Perry D. Slocum'
FLOWER COLOR: changeable
MATURE FLOWER SIZE: 9-12 inches across
BLOOM TIME: summer
MATURE PLANT HEIGHT: 4-5 square feet
LEAF SIZE: 15-24 inches

For a long-lasting flower display, 'Momo Botan' is unrivaled among lotuses. Its flowers remain open later in the day than many of its peers and for several days longer, too. Sometimes new ones are emerging while mature ones are still lingering on, making for a varied and breathtaking display. The blooming season also exceeds that of most other lotuses. In all, it's unbeatable!

This lotus really does need several weeks in the 80s in order to bloom. Your reward is truly lovely, full blossoms, rosy pink with a glowing yellow interior; they radiate an enchanting, sweet scent. Seed capsules are also small and attractive.

Luckily, this excellent plant is also suitable for smaller water gardens or half-barrel or kettle displays.

For sheer magnificence, 'Mrs. Perry D. Slocum' is tops. The large flowers are plentiful and richly fragrant, with a scent that has been likened to anise or sweet licorice. They begin strawberry pink, then a light buttery yellow emerges; by the third day, the petals are creamy white suffused with soft peach-pink. At any given time, you may find blooms in different stages on the same plant. (Later, the seed capsules put on a color show, too. They start yellow, become green, and then dry a brown color.)

With such big flowers and large, towering leaves, this lotus is not for the small pool. Put it in a really big container (a shallow plastic kiddy pool, even, something 3 or 4 feet across and a foot or so deep) in a large pool and watch the amazing show unfurl.

LOTUS

Perry's Giant Sunburst
Nelumbo 'Perry's Giant Sunburst'
FLOWER COLOR: pale yellow
MATURE FLOWER SIZE: 10-13 inches across
BLOOM TIME: summer
MATURE PLANT HEIGHT: 4$^{1}/_{2}$-5$^{1}/_{2}$ square feet
LEAF SIZE: 16-18 inches

One of this lotus's parents is the yellow *Nelumbo lutea*, which no doubt accounts for its softer hue of yellow. The outer petals are lime-green, further enhancing the elegant beauty. These are big, magnificent blossoms, held high above the large leaves. Even the seed capsules are gorgeous, beginning yellow, then lime-yellow with a green rim, then entirely green, before finally drying brown.

Such a big plant requires a big pot and a big pool, but if you are able to provide these growing conditions, you will have a real showpiece.

Red Scarf
Nelumbo 'Red Scarf'
FLOWER COLOR: pink
MATURE FLOWER SIZE: 3-6 inches across
BLOOM TIME: summer
MATURE PLANT HEIGHT: 1$^{1}/_{2}$-2$^{1}/_{2}$ square feet
LEAF SIZE: 10-15 inches

This utterly charming relative newcomer to the lotus scene is small, technically "semi-dwarf." The pretty petals are more hot pink than red, despite the name, with a yellow center seed capsule. The flowers hold up very well in hot, humid weather.

Grow this vivacious little lotus in a tub garden or smaller pool.

PLANT DIRECTORY: CAN'T MISS WATER GARDEN FAVORITES   **151**

Marginal Plants

a ny plant that prospers in shallow water is considered a marginal, or emergent, plant, and is suitable for a water garden. Shorter ones are nice to add to container displays. These add height, texture, and interest to any water garden, with and without blooms. (They are also practical, deriving nutrients from the water that might otherwise be used to nurture algae.)

Many are enthusiastic growers and should be confined to a pot. This not only contains their spread, but also makes tinkering with the overall design possible. Most will thrive immersed in no more than 6 inches of water; even shallower is better. Full sun exposure is ideal. Keep them groomed and fertilize regularly.

Please note: Some marginals are invasive, aggressive growers. You can still grow them, where legal but you must raise each one in a pot. You must also dispose of prunings (or entire plants) safely, that is, in your yard (your compost pile is perfect), *never* in man-made or natural waterways where the plant can become a pest or compete with native plants.

Many are perfectly winter-hardy. So they can go in the pool earlier in spring and stay in later in the fall. If you wish, and if your winters are not too harsh, they can spend the entire winter in the water—with a little advance preparation (basically, cutting them back and placing them underwater in the deepest part of the pool). Alternatively, you can take them out and keep them indoors in a cool, nonfreezing place.

As for marginals of tropical origin, they must be removed from the water in fall and kept in a protected, nonfreezing location indoors until the following season. Or you can discard them and get new ones next spring. Don't just leave them in the water, as they will die and add detrimental decaying organic matter. For details, consult Chapter 3.

Arrowhead, Duck Potato
Sagittaria latifolia
MATURE FLOWER SIZE: 1^{1}/$_{2}$-2 inches
FLOWER COLOR: white
BLOOM TIME: summer
MATURE PLANT SIZE: 2-4 feet H x W
HARDINESS ZONES: 4 or 5-11

It grows easily, flowers readily, and looks nice with other water-garden plants, including waterlilies. The bright green, three-pointed leaves are arrowhead-shaped; the perky little three-petaled flowers are carried on stalks among them.

This plant grows from small tubers, and its pot may be submerged in as little as an inch of water and perhaps as much as a foot. Cover the potted plant's surface with gravel, to prevent the soil from drifting into the pool and to discourage ducks and other waterfowl that relish the tasty tubers.

GOOD CHOICES: 'Crushed Ice' is a variety with cream-and-green variegated foliage. Other, similar species are also available. The awl-leaved arrowhead, *Sagittaria subulata*, has some larger submerged leaves and smaller floating leaves. Japanese arrowhead, *Sagittaria sagittifolia*, has purple-marked flowers and can be invasive; its cultivar 'Flore Pleno' is said to be less aggressive and has huge white pom-pom flowers. Aztec or giant arrowhead, *S. montevidensis*, is treasured for its beautiful red-accented, pure-white flowers and is hardy in Zones 8-10.

Canna
Canna x *generalis*
MATURE FLOWER SIZE: 4-6 inches
FLOWER COLOR: varies
BLOOM TIME: midsummer
MATURE PLANT SIZE: 2-8 feet H x 1-3 feet W
HARDINESS ZONES: 6 or 7-10

For tropical pizzazz in your water garden, water-loving cannas deliver—in style. They are quite tall and have large, banana-like leaves. The sensational blossoms appear starting in midsummer and come in a range of bright colors and bicolors, primarily red, hot pink, orange, and yellow. Those with reddish, bronze, striped, or variegated leaves are assets even when the plants are not blooming.

Give these showy plants full sun, large pots (for their roots and also for stability), and frequent fertilizing. As for placement, because they are so tall and large, give them a background position, a corner, or a spot out in the center—anywhere where they can be well admired without blocking the view of lower-growers. Cannas have even proven to be hardy for many gardeners in Zone 6.

GOOD CHOICES: Any in the Longwood series (which are floriferous and shorter, 2 to 3 feet) are good, including red 'Endeavour', salmon 'Erebus', and yellow 'Ra'. Fiery-orange-flowered 'Pretoria' has sensational variegated leaves.

Cattail
Typha species
MATURE FLOWER SIZE: varies
FLOWER COLOR: brown
BLOOM TIME: late summer
MATURE PLANT SIZE: 2-6 feet H x 1-3 feet W
HARDINESS ZONES: 3-11

This is a water garden classic with a surprising number of choices. The brown flower heads appear later in summer, but the vertical foliage is a handsome contribution to your display all season. They are easy to grow and compatible with other marginals and waterlilies and a great addition to any naturalistic water garden.

For best results, grow your cattails in substantial pots and immerse them in a few inches of water (for the largest ones, no more than a foot). It's important to keep them contained, as they are vigorous growers. To prevent seedlings (especially if you live near a natural area), cut off flower heads before the fluffy seeds start to disperse.

GOOD CHOICES: Tall narrow-leaf cattail, *Typha angustifolia* reaches 4 to 6 feet; a dwarf specied (only 14 inches high!) is *Typha minima*. In-between options include *T. laxmannii*, whose handsome and graceful blue-green leaves top out around 2 or 4 feet; and *T. latifolia* 'Variegata', which grows 4 to 5 feet high and has twisted leaves featuring broad bands of green and white.

Golden Club
Orontium aquaticum
MATURE FLOWER SIZE: 4-6 inches
FLOWER COLOR: yellow
BLOOM TIME: spring to early summer
MATURE PLANT SIZE: 1 foot H x 1 1/2 feet W
HARDINESS ZONES: 6-11

The foliage—upright-reaching, oval, blue-green leaves up to a foot long—is good looking, but not especially exciting. The flowers, on the other hand, are very intriguing, and make quite a show early in the growing season. They're actually thin white spikes tipped with gold, and reach 4 or more inches high.

This plant is a welcome addition to pools where early color is desired, before the waterlilies and other aquatics really hit their stride; grow it in moist soil or immerse it 6 or so inches deep. In and out of bloom, it looks terrific in combination with the water iris. Overall, it is an easy plant, free of pests and diseases and always looking crisp. It tolerates shade well, too.

GOOD CHOICES: (no variations)

Iris

Iris species and hybrids

MATURE FLOWER SIZE: 2-6 inches
FLOWER COLOR: varies
BLOOM TIME: early spring to midsummer
MATURE PLANT SIZE: 1-3 feet H x 1-2 feet W
HARDINESS ZONES: 4-9, in most cases

For sheer flower color power, no other moisture-loving plant beats the iris. The only drawback—many irises bloom for only two weeks. But for their period of glory, they are truly fabulous. For an extended bloom season, plant different species.

Irises have handsome, strap-like or spear-shaped foliage that is untroubled by nibbling pests. This quality will keep the plants valuable after the flowers are long past. Irises also turn out to be good filter plants, meaning they take nutrients from the water and thereby contribute to keeping it clearer.

Immerse potted iris plants in one-gallon pots in shallow water, generally 6 inches deep or less. Full sun is best.

GOOD CHOICES: All the Louisiana irises are suitable for water displays; gorgeous 'Black Gamecock', royal purple with flashy golden accents; 'Delta Dawn', pretty pink. Pale blue *I. versicolor* and *I. virginica* and the rusty-colored copper iris (*I. fulva*) are native to the U.S. Siberian iris (*I. sibirica*). Japanese iris (*I. ensata*, syn. *I. kaempferi*), and *I. laevigata* are also good choices.

Lizard's Tail

Saururus cernuus

MATURE FLOWER SIZE: 6-inch spikes
FLOWER COLOR: white
BLOOM TIME: summer
MATURE PLANT SIZE: 1-3 feet H x 1-2 feet W
HARDINESS ZONES: 4-9

A shorter plant, best suited to the edges of a pool or a container water garden, lizard's tail forms attractive clumps. The heart-shaped leaves are apple green and about 2 feet tall. Lots of slender, nodding spikes of creamy white flowers arch above them in midsummer. These waft a faintly sweet, citrusy fragrance. Slightly puckered greenish fruits follow; their arrangement along the curving stalk might have inspired the common name.

It is best in a pot of rich soil, immersed no more than 6 inches deep.

GOOD CHOICES: The similar Chinese lizard's tail, *Saururus chinensis*, has a white blotch on the topmost leaf, helping the plant to stand out even more, especially in part shade.

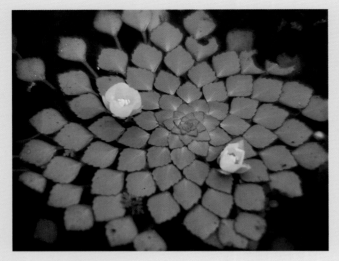

Mosaic Plant
Ludwigia sedioides
MATURE FLOWER SIZE: 1 inch
FLOWER COLOR: yellow
BLOOM TIME: late summer
MATURE PLANT SIZE: 1/2 inch H x spreading
HARDINESS ZONES: 9-10

Papyrus, Umbrella Palm
Cyperus species and cultivars
MATURE FLOWER SIZE: tiny seedheads
FLOWER COLOR: green-brown
BLOOM TIME: summer
MATURE PLANT SIZE: H x W vary
HARDINESS ZONES: 8-10

Just gorgeous! Floating leaves composed of dozens of tiny diamond shapes look as though someone has tossed a handful of emeralds into your pool. The stems are reddish, and the leaves may gain a reddish tinge. The plant expands by sending up additional rosettes. In very warm weather, it may be inspired to flower, displaying the occasional tiny yellow blossom. But the real show is the beautiful, intriguing foliage.

Pot *Ludwigia sedioides* (syn. *Ludwigia stellata*) in soil, and immerse it in at least 4 inches of water. The foliage will make it to the surface and remain all season long, delighting everyone who beholds it. This is also a lovely choice for a water display in a small container.

Warning: This plant is not a good choice if you keep koi, because they find it delicious!

GOOD CHOICES: (there are no variations)

This is actually a large group of plants, with plenty of variety in size and height. Their green leaves are stiff and triangular, and the plant is vertical and upright. Tufts of brownish flowers surrounded by what are technically whorls of spiked foliage in greenish hues add heft.

The biggest one—reaching a towering 6 feet or more—is the Egyptian paper reed, *Cyperus papyrus*, once used in paper-making. At the other end of the scale is the "dwarf" papyrus, *C. haspan*, at a mere 30 inches. In between is the ever-popular umbrella palm, *C. alternifolius*, which gets to about 3 to 5 feet. All aid in water clarity by consuming nutrients in the water that might otherwise nurture unwanted algae. In cooler areas, any *Cyperus* can be overwintered indoors as a houseplant.

GOOD CHOICES: An especially desirable variation is *C. alternifolius* 'Variegatus', which is shorter and has lengthwise white stripes. A nice, compact edition is *C. involucratus* 'Nanus', which stays about 2 feet high.

Pickerel Rush, Pickerel Weed
Pontederia cordata
MATURE FLOWER SIZE: 3-6 inches
FLOWER COLOR: blue, purple, white
BLOOM TIME: midsummer to fall
MATURE PLANT SIZE: 18-30 inches H x 12-18 inches W
HARDINESS ZONES: 3-11

A handsome, easy-going plant, this clump-former has lance-shaped leaves up to 3 feet long. They are joined in midsummer by wonderful blue to purple flower spikes that continue well into fall. Dragonflies and butterflies adore them.

Pickerel rush is splendid in combination with the yellow or pink flowers of many waterlilies and marginals, but not as satisfactory with other blue flowers because the color is hard to match. There is a more versatile white version, and occasionally a nursery has the pink-flowered edition, which is pretty.

Grow this marginal in a sturdy one-gallon pot, set in shallow water or up to 10 inches below the water's surface.

GOOD CHOICES: *Pontederia cordata alba*, which isn't quite as hardy, is the white-spiked version. 'Pink Pons' in pink.

Spike Rush, Fiber-optic Plant
Eleocharis montevidensis
MATURE FLOWER SIZE: $1/4$ inch
FLOWER COLOR: brown
BLOOM TIME: summer
MATURE PLANT SIZE: 12 inches H x 6-12 inches W
HARDINESS ZONES: 6-11

This is a perky little clump-forming accent plant, ideal for pool's edge or a container water garden, usually reaching no more than a foot or so high. It sports slender but erect leaves that are tipped with tiny brown "flower" nubs.

Grow spike rush in a 1-gallon pot in shallow water, no more than an inch or two deep. It grows quickly to size, but is not rampant or invasive when confined to a pot.

GOOD CHOICES: The related Chinese water chestnut, *Eleocharis tuberosa*, grows taller, to 30 inches, has bigger spikelets, and is not as hardy (Zones 7-11; overwinter indoors in colder areas).

MARGINAL PLANTS

Striped Rush, Soft Twig Rush
Machaerina rubiginosa
MATURE FLOWER SIZE: tiny spikelets
FLOWER COLOR: reddish-brown
BLOOM TIME: summer (if it blooms)
MATURE PLANT SIZE: 18-24 inches H x 6-12 inches W
HARDINESS ZONES: 7-11

From Australia comes this reedlike plant with cylindrical leaf blades. It is relatively new to cultivation and gaining in popularity because it is so attractive and reliable. It grows fairly slowly—which many water gardeners consider a plus—and is suitable for small to medium-sized pools. It may also be raised in a tub display. Striped rush, *Machaerina rubiginosa* (syn. *Baumea rubiginosa*), is best in full sun and immersed 1 to no more than 6 inches below the water surface.

GOOD CHOICES: Handsome 'Variegata' grows to 2 feet, with gold vertically striped blades.

Sweet Flag, Japanese Rush
Acorus calumus
MATURE FLOWER SIZE: 2 inches
FLOWER COLOR: brown
BLOOM TIME: midsummer
MATURE PLANT SIZE: 2-4 feet H x 1-2 feet W
HARDINESS ZONES: 4-11

An iris relative, this grassy-leaved plant is appreciated not for its flowers (which aren't anything to write home about, small brownish hornlike things) but for its reliably attractive foliage. The leaves grow in dense bunches and are strappy, bright green with distinct midribs and occasionally wrinkled margins. They are lightly scented, a pleasant, citrusy smell.

For the best show, however, you want to seek out the variegated-leaf versions of this plant. Longitudinal stripes of white or cream add a lot of appeal.

Grow sweet flag in moist soil or shallow water (smaller ones about 3 inches deep, taller ones up to 6 inches deep), and avoid disturbing the roots once planted.

GOOD CHOICES: 'Variegatus' is the classic, cream-striped edition; it may also be shorter than the species. *Acorus gramineus* 'Ogon', or dwarf sweet flag, is somewhat shorter, to 10 inches, with pale-green and cream stripes.

Taro, Elephant's Ear
Colocasia esculenta
MATURE FLOWER SIZE: small spathes (rare)
FLOWER COLOR: white
BLOOM TIME: summer
MATURE PLANT SIZE: 2-6 feet H x 2-4 feet W
HARDINESS ZONES: 9-11

Water Canna
Thalia dealbata
MATURE FLOWER SIZE: $1/2$-$3/4$ inch in 8-inch panicles
FLOWER COLOR: blue-purple
BLOOM TIME: summer
MATURE PLANT SIZE: 2-6 feet H x W
HARDINESS ZONES: 6-11

Spectacular tropical foliage plants, taros have big heart-shaped leaves reaching 3 or more feet. These shed water the way lotus leaves do, and may be marked with purple or cranberry red or have contrasting margins or veins. They do just fine with less light.

Taro plants grow from a tuber. Plant each one several inches deep in an ample pot, without covering the growing tip. Set it in moist soil or up to 6 inches of water. Fertilizing inspires lusher growth.

In Zone 8 and colder, you can treat it like a houseplant over the winter—or the tuber can be dried and stored in a non-freezing place. Prepare it for storage if temperatures are going to fall below 50 degrees F. (Properly prepared, the tubers are used in certain Asian dishes.)

GOOD CHOICES: The very popular 'Black Magic' has dark purple, nearly black, leaves and stems. 'Illustris' has gorgeous blue-black leaves and thick green veining, and it attains about 3 feet in height.

Somewhat similar to its tropical canna cousins, hardy water canna has graceful, oblong, blue-green leaves. Small but pretty flowers are carried on long, arching stalks and are generally light blue to purple (with a hint of silver for extra sparkle). The plant grows to between 2 and 6 feet, so site its big presence where it won't block the view of your lower-growing plants. It looks terrific in combination with *Cyperus*.

A plant this big and exuberant requires a big pot so it won't tip over. Set the pot in the water no more than a foot deep.

GOOD CHOICES: The subspecies *ruminoides* has gorgeous red stems—a real showpiece! Alligator flag, *Thalia geniculata*, is similar but not as hardy (Zones 9 to 10—it will not survive a frost)—it gets its name, as you might guess, from the fact that alligators cruising under the water's surface inadvertently give away their location when the flower stalks move in response to their passing!

Water Celery, Water Parsley
Oenanthe javanica
MATURE FLOWER SIZE: 1/8 inch
FLOWER COLOR: white
BLOOM TIME: summer
MATURE PLANT SIZE: 6-12 inches H x spreading
HARDINESS ZONES: 5-11

As the name suggests, this attractive marginal is also an edible plant. The finely cut foliage does resemble celery and has a mild peppery flavor, suitable for salads and stuffing. Using the trimmings in summer meals, actually, would be a good way to make use of them. The flower heads are white and lacy, when they appear.

This is a nice looking plant, suitable for pond edges, where it does a good job of hiding exposed edges or stonework. It's also good in container displays. Either way, set the pot in moist soil or up to 5 inches or so of water. It is another good filter plant (extracts nutrients from the water, helping to keep it clearer).

GOOD CHOICES: The beautiful cultivar 'Flamingo' is widely available and preferred for its colorfulness; the light green foliage is edged in cream or pink or both. Coloration is best in full sun.

Water Clover
Marsilea mutica
MATURE FLOWER SIZE: none—reproduces via spores
FLOWER COLOR: none
BLOOM TIME: none
MATURE PLANT SIZE: up to 6 inches H x spreading
HARDINESS ZONES: 6-11

Each little four-leaved water-clover plant is a mere 3 inches across, with accents of white, yellow, or bronze. A fern relative, there are no flowers. It does best in still water and forms small mat-like colonies. In the evenings and on overcast days, the leaves sometimes fold up to look like tiny butterflies at rest. The leaves tend to float on the water surface, but will rear up when overgrown or crowded. Fish seek shelter under the foliage.

To control its growth, water clover must be potted (never grow it loose or it will take over!) and may be immersed in up to 4 inches of water. There's no need to fertilize.

GOOD CHOICES: The cultivar 'Micro Mini' is even smaller than the species, with leaves about a half-inch across. Hairy water clover, *Marsilea drummondii*, has silvery foliage and is somewhat bigger than *M. mutica*. Upright water clover, *M. quadrifolia*, has upright, triangular leaves. Butterfly water clover, *M. rotundifolia*, has 1-inch leaves that open and close daily.

Water Poppy
Hydrocleys nymphoides
MATURE FLOWER SIZE: 2 inches
FLOWER COLOR: yellow
BLOOM TIME: summer
MATURE PLANT SIZE: 2-4 inches H x up to 6 feet W
HARDINESS ZONES: 9-11

This is a bold plant both in appearance and in growing habits, and so is best used in larger pools. The 2-inch, three-petaled, cup-shaped flowers do indeed resemble bright yellow poppies and are produced in profusion above a mass of shiny green, oval leaves. This plant is particularly splendid in the company of yellow waterlilies.

Place a pot of this lusty grower in a few inches, but no more than a foot, of water. You must keep after it, trimming off unwanted stems and spent flowers as the season progresses.

GOOD CHOICES: Giant water poppy, *Hydrocleys peruviana*, is identical but grows even larger.

Water Snowflake
Nymphoides indica
MATURE FLOWER SIZE: 1 1/2 inches
FLOWER COLOR: white
BLOOM TIME: summer
MATURE PLANT SIZE: 2 inches H x spreading
HARDINESS ZONES: 8-11

Adorable, and aptly named! Green leaves that look just like mini lilypads float on the water's surface, all on their own a nice addition to any pool; they're generally about 5 inches across, but they can get bigger. The perky little flowers that soon join them, rising a bit above the surface, sport five frilly, highly fringed white petals. The plant starts blooming in spring and continues all summer long!

Grow this charmer in a pot that is immersed several inches to 1 foot or so. The leaves and flowers will work their way to the surface. A nice choice for a small container, especially if a full-sized waterlily is not possible.

GOOD CHOICES: Australian snowflake, *Nymphoides cristata*, has smaller leaves edged and marked burgundy and smaller, half-inch white flowers. Yellow snowflake, *N. geminata*, has darker green leaves with bright green veining and 1-inch yellow flowers.

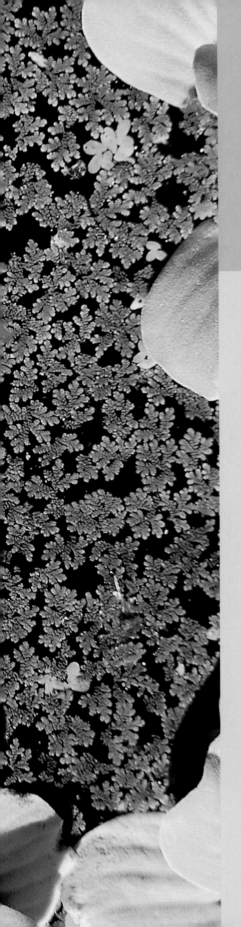

Floaters and Submerged Plants

These plants can be a pleasant and low-maintenance addition to your display. Either simply toss them in the water, or pot them up in order to anchor them. They grow easily—sometimes too easily, which means you may be hauling some out from time to time (see note below about disposing of these safely).

Floaters are welcome because they help fulfill the requirement of two-thirds water coverage that leads to a healthy pool, plus they provide shelter for fish and use nutrients that might otherwise feed unwanted amounts of algae.

Submerged plants can fill a similar role, or just hang out under the water. In years past, they were often billed as "oxygenating plants." This moniker has gone out of popular usage because it is only partially true—they do the important work of creating oxygen underwater during the sunny daylight hours only. If you peer in, you may observe tiny bubbles percolating from their foliage into the surrounding water.

Please note: Some floaters and submerged plants, noted in their description, are considered invasive, aggressive growers in mild climates. You can still grow them, where legal, but you must dispose of prunings (or entire plants) safely, that is, in your yard (your compost pile is perfect), never in man-made or natural waterways where they can become a pest or compete with native plants.

Tropical or hardy, floaters and submerged plants are so prolific and so inexpensive, there's no need to trouble yourself with their survival.

They should not be left in the water over the winter months, as they will die and break down, adding detrimental organic matter to the pool. So try to scoop them out in the fall and dispose of them properly—on your compost pile is best. If you'd like to save some for next year, keep a few (you won't need many) indoors in a heated aquarium.

Note: If you don't know your USDA Hardiness Zone, find your location on the map on page 166.

Duckweed
Lemna minor

MATURE FLOWER SIZE: tiny
FLOWER COLOR: green
BLOOM TIME: early summer
MATURE PLANT SIZE: $1/8$ inch **H** x even smaller **W**
HARDINESS ZONES: 3-11

Sometimes called "the world's smallest plant," tiny duckweed travels or gathers in clumps. Each individual plant has roots hanging below its lime-green, oval-shaped leaves. This allows the plant to float freely in your pool or container garden, getting whatever nutrition it may need right from the water. You rarely need to buy it—it tends to hitchhike in on other water plants. If it reproduces too vigorously, just discard handfuls on your compost pile. It's not really a pest, though, and besides, goldfish and koi like to nibble it, so it's good to have around for that reason alone. In fact, fish will often start eating it right away, thus keeping the duckweed population under control. (Ducks like it, too, of course.)

Eelgrass, Tape Grass
Vallisneria spiralis

MATURE FLOWER SIZE: insignificant
FLOWER COLOR: pale green
BLOOM TIME: rare in cultivation
MATURE PLANT SIZE: 3- 6 feet **H** x $1/2$ inch **W**
HARDINESS ZONES: 8-11

This one has long, narrow leaves. It's useful in the pool for water quality, for oxygen, and as habitat for fish. Another common name, spiral tape grass, refers to the spiraling nature of the flower stalks. Male and female plants are separate. Flower stalks of male plants separate from the plant and leave pollen on the water surface; the female flower stalks grow to the surface to retrieve it, and then contract so seeds ripen underwater. *Vallisneria gigantea*, a native of South America, has longer and wider leaves. *Vallisneria americana* has leaves up to 3 feet long and is hardier (Zones 4-10), though it can be vigorous.

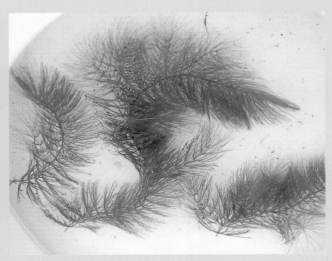

Fairy Moss
Azolla filiculoides
MATURE FLOWER SIZE: does not bloom
FLOWER COLOR: does not bloom
BLOOM TIME: does not bloom
MATURE PLANT SIZE: $3/8$ inch H x spreading
HARDINESS ZONES: 5-10

Not technically a moss, this tiny but rampant grower is actually an aquatic fern. Two-lobed, fuzzy leaves on short stems float freely on the water surface, forming small colonies. As they age, the leaves gain a reddish tint. Full sun and cool temperatures also inspire the reddish coloration.

This is a good floater to add to your display when you need quick surface coverage. But once that's attained, you'll need to thin periodically. In the wild, its buds fall to the pond bottom to overwinter, returning with a vengeance the following year. This is apparently not a problem in water gardens.

Azolla filiculoides (syn. *Azolla caroliniana*) can be invasive, so never dispose of it near waterways.

Hornwort
Ceratophyllum demersum
MATURE FLOWER SIZE: tiny/insignificant
FLOWER COLOR: pale green
BLOOM TIME: rarely flowers in cultivation
MATURE PLANT SIZE: 1-2 feet H x trailing
HARDINESS ZONES: 6-10

You may have seen this one in aquariums, and it makes a fine transition to an outdoor water garden. Once you drop it in the pool, it remains underwater, neither floating on the surface nor sinking right to the bottom—oddly enough, it can exist without developing any roots, though in some situations it will loosely anchor itself to the bottom of a pond. During winter, it drops down to lower depths. It can be used in still or moving water, so it would work in ponds with fountains.

Fish often seek shelter in hornwort's whorls of thin, needlelike, branched foliage, or even spawn within its bounds. Koi tend not to bother it.

Parrot's Feather
Myriophyllum aquaticum
MATURE FLOWER SIZE: tiny/not significant
FLOWER COLOR: yellow-green
BLOOM TIME: summer
MATURE PLANT SIZE: $^1/_2$-2+ feet H x spreading
HARDINESS ZONES: 6-11

Bright green, unbranched stems are lined with feathery whorls of leaves (up to 3 inches in diameter!). There is a dwarf, red-stemmed variety that is gaining popularity because its growth is more compact and manageable—the name is *M. proserpinacoides*. Another compact type is *M. heterophyllum.*

A handsome, vigorous plant, parrot's feather is not content to remain underwater and may poke its head out or even trail over your display's edges (or the rim of its container, if you grow it in one). It shelters baby fish (fry) and also does well in deep water pools. In any event, though, you must keep after it, tearing out excess growth.

Parrot's feather is invasive and is banned in Washington, New Hampshire, Maine, Vermont, Nevada, and Alabama.

Water Lettuce
Pistia stratiotes
MATURE FLOWER SIZE: tiny, not significant
FLOWER COLOR: pale green-white
BLOOM TIME: summer
MATURE PLANT SIZE: 4 inches H x 8 inches W
HARDINESS ZONES: 8-11

The handsome, textured leaves of water lettuce invite touching—they are soft and velvety and, like those of lotus and taro, shed droplets of water when splashed. The rosettes float merrily on the water surface, forming dense colonies over time. Fish spawn in the especially long, dangling roots that trail below.

Water lettuce can be sensitive to too much direct sun (which causes the leaves to turn yellow and/or have burnt brown edges), so it is best used in containers or pools that don't receive all-day sun.

Water lettuce can be invasive, so dispose of it properly. It is banned in California, Texas, Louisiana, South Carolina, Alabama, and Florida.

usda cold hardiness zones

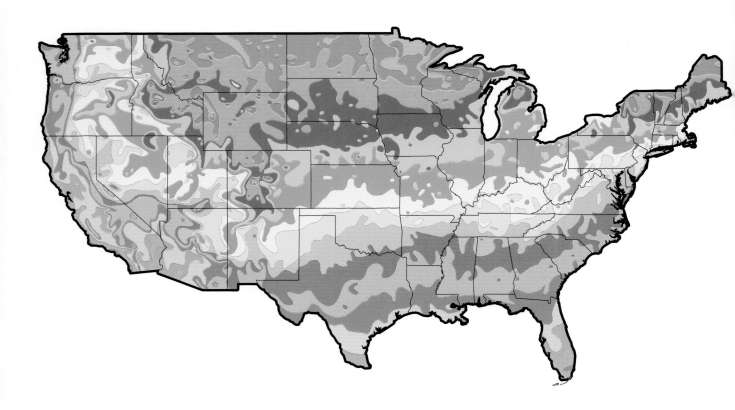

ZONE	Average Annual Minimum Temperature (°F)
2B	-40 to -45
3A	-35 to -40
3B	-30 to -35
4A	-25 to -30
4B	-20 to -25
5A	-15 to -20

ZONE	Average Annual Minimum Temperature (°F)
5B	-10 to -15
6A	-5 to -10
6B	0 to -5
7A	5 to 0
7B	10 to 5
8A	15 to 10

ZONE	Average Annual Minimum Temperature (°F)
8B	20 to 15
9A	25 to 20
9B	30 to 25
10A	35 to 30
10B	40 to 35
11	40 and Above

seasonal checklist

Spring

- ☐ Begin feeding your fish when water temperature climbs over 50 degrees F.
- ☐ Using a net, scoop out decaying organic material (a general after-winter clean up).
- ☐ Test pump, test filter.
- ☐ Inspect pool (liner) for damage such as nicks and small leaks, and repair as necessary.
- ☐ Make sure stones/edging materials are stable.
- ☐ Divide and repot overgrown plants.
- ☐ Repot tropical waterlilies for a fresh start.
- ☐ Scoop out and discard toad and frog eggs.
- ☐ Remove decaying leaves and spent blossoms now.
- ☐ Retrieve hardy plants that overwintered in the bottom of the pool, and clean or repot as necessary—then return to the pool at proper depths.
- ☐ Retrieve hardy plants that overwintered indoors, assess viability, and divide or repot as necessary—then place in the pool after the water temperature climbs over 50 degrees F.
- ☐ Pot up new mail-order plants as they arrive.
- ☐ Order new plants and/or visit garden centers that have good water-garden sections.

Summer

- ☐ Fertilize waterlilies and lotus twice a month. (More-robust marginals may not need feeding.)
- ☐ Remove decaying leaves and spent blossoms now.
- ☐ Carefully check plants for signs of pests.
- ☐ Top off pool as needed due to evaporation.
- ☐ Collect viviparous plants from lilypads as they appear and try starting new plants.
- ☐ Scoop out excess algae.
- ☐ Prune rampant plants—dispose of plants and trimmings properly (never in man-made or natural waterways!).

- ☐ Feed fish once or twice a day (only as much as they will consume in five minutes).
- ☐ If midday sun is causing certain waterlilies to flag or their color to fade too fast, offer some shade (even an umbrella will help).
- ☐ Pot up new mail-order plants as they arrive.
- ☐ If necessary, take steps to protect plants and fish from marauding wildlife.
- ☐ Check pump and filter through the season; clean filters regularly.

Fall

- ☐ Skim leaves and debris out of the pond (place a protective netting over the surface if necessary).
- ☐ Reduce, and then cease fertilizing of plants.
- ☐ Reduce feeding of fish (and cease completely if the water temperature drops below 50 degrees F).
- ☐ Divide overgrown plants and repot.
- ☐ Clean pump inlet screens. Clean filter. (Safely store these items indoors if necessary.)
- ☐ Install a new pond? Weather is cooler/less chance of algal bloom.
- ☐ If frost threatens, remove tropical and tender plants and keep indoors (see Chapter 3).

Winter

- ☐ Take steps to prevent surface from freezing (see Chapter 3).
- ☐ If mildest areas, you may let pump run continuously (raise up a bit so as not to stir up bottom).
- ☐ If frost threatens, remove tropical and tender plants and keep indoors.
- ☐ Keep pond area clear of debris.
- ☐ Order new plants from catalogs or Web sites.
- ☐ Occasionally check on plants that are overwintering indoors; if rot is obvious, you may discard, but if in doubt, wait till spring to assess.

resources

Mail-Order Suppliers

Green & Hagstrom
P.O. Box 658
7767 Fernvale Rd.
Fairview, TN 37062
www.greenandhagstrom.com

Hardwicke Gardens
254 Boston Turnpike Rd./Rte. 9 East
Westborough, MA 01581
www.hardwickegardens.com

LilyBlooms Aquatic Gardens
932 South Main St.
North Canton, OH 44720
www.lilyblooms.com

Lilypons Water Gardens
6800 Lilypons Rd.
P.O. Box 10
Buckeystown, MD 21717-0010
www.lilypons.com

Perry's Water Gardens
136 Gibson Aquatic Farm Rd.
Franklin, NC 28734-0444
www.perryswatergarden.net

The Pond Guy
6135 King Rd.
Marine City, MI 48039
www.thepondguy.com

Ponds.com
P.O. Box 5564
Saginaw, MI 48603
www.eponds.com

S. Scherer & Sons, Inc.
104 Waterside Rd.
Northport, NY 11768
www.waterlilyfarm.com

Tilley's Nursery/The Water Works
111 E. Fairmont St.
Coppersburg, PA 18036
www.tnwaterworks.com

Van Ness Water Gardens
2460 North Euclid Ave.
Upland, CA 91784-1199
www.vnwg.com

The Water Garden
5212 Austin Rd.
Chattanooga, TN 37343
www.watergarden.com

Water Tropicals
P.O. Box 211574
Royal Palm Beach, FL 33421
www.watertropicals.com

Waterford Gardens
74 East Allendale Rd.
Saddle River, NJ 07458
www.waterfordgardens.com

National Clubs, Societies, and Organizations

Aquatic Gardeners Association
P.O. Box 51536
Denton, TX 76206
www.aquatic-gardeners.org

Associated Koi Clubs of America
www.akca.org
Consult the website for the nearest branch of this national club.

International Waterlily and Water Gardening Society
6828 26th St. W.
Bradenton, FL 34207
www.iwgs.org

Specialty Magazines

There is only one—but it is terrific!

Water Gardening: The Magazine for Pondkeepers
P.O. Box 607
St. John, IN 46373
$24.99 for one year; $39.99 for two years; $59.99 for three years
www.watergardening.com

Public Displays

Below is a list of gardens open to the public that include water-garden displays. These are well worth visiting, camera and notebook in hand, if you are lucky to live nearby or happen to be traveling in the area. You'll gain valuable, practical information about aquatic plants and how they grow, as well as get inspiration from the design of the displays. Because most water gardens are at their best in summer, that's the best time to go.

Some of these places also involve volunteers in caring for the displays, a great way to learn and to meet other water gardeners. And some have wonderful annual plant sales, where you can get quality plants to take home—popular favorites as well as the occasional rarity.

Atlanta Botanical Garden
Atlanta, GA

Denver Botanic Gardens
Denver, CO

Ganna Walska Lotusland
Montecito, CA

Longwood Gardens
Kennett Square, PA

Mercer Arboretum and Botanic Gardens
Humble, TX

Missouri Botanical Garden
St. Louis, MO

New York Botanical Garden
Bronx, NY

Local Resources

Your best bet is to check your current Yellow Pages under "Pools" or "Pond" or "Water Features" or "Landscape Services—Water Gardens." Or inquire at your nearest or largest garden center to see if they can refer you to specialized help.

As for garden clubs that specialize in water gardening, these are constantly popping up (and occasionally merging or going defunct). Ask around to see if there's one in your area—good ways to find one include asking at the place where you buy water plants and supplies, asking someone who already has a water feature in their yard, or attending an advertised talk on water gardening. Local societies are a terrific way to get ideas, information, and social interaction with other water gardeners. You may also get a chance to go on inspiring pond tours or participate in plant swaps!

plant index

meet the author

Teri Dunn

Teri Dunn is a freelance writer and editor. She is the author of *Can't Miss Flower Gardening* and co-author of *Can't Miss Container Gardening*, as well as numerous other gardening titles, including *Jackson & Perkins Beautiful Roses Made Easy; Jackson & Perkins Selecting, Growing, and Combining Perennials; Potting Places: Creative Ideas for Practical Gardening Workspaces; Cottage Gardens; 600 Garden Favorites;* and several books in the popular *100 Favorites* series, including roses, perennials, herbs, shade plants, and others. She resides on Cape Ann, Massachusetts, with her husband, Shawn, sons Wes and Tristan, and dog Buddy.